Operatic Divas
and
Naked Irishmen

Published 2017
Printed in the United States of America
ISBN: 978 1 63152 194 2 pbk
ISBN: 978-1-63152-195-9 ebk
Library of Congress Control Number: 2017930641

Cover design by Rebecca Lown
Interior design by Tabitha Lahr

For information, address:
She Writes Press
1563 Solano Ave #546
Berkeley, CA 94707

She Writes Press is a division of SparkPoint Studio, LLC.

Operatic Divas
and
Naked Irishmen

AN INNKEEPER'S TALE

Nancy Hinchliff

SHE WRITES PRESS

For my daughters, with love,
who supported and helped me
from beginning to the end.
Thank you.

Chapter 1

THE BIG MOVE

The movers slammed the heavy doors together and walked around to the front of the van. I watched from my third-floor apartment window as they climbed up into the cab. Then I started toward the front door. It was June 1995, eight months before I would open my bed and breakfast. My furniture was in the moving van, and I was packed and ready to leave Chicago.

Glancing back into the apartment, I could hear the faint squeals of my three-year-old grandson, as though he were there. The sounds drifted down the hallway and past the empty bookcase where the stereo used to be. It still sat against one wall, too heavy and too large to take to Louisville. In the dim light, my imagination conjured up images of the two of us twirling and laughing, mesmerized by the music, as we danced to his favorite nursery rhyme. *E-I-E-I-O* echoed through the quiet of the morning.

I loved this place, and I hated leaving Chicago, and this apartment. Large windows covered two walls in the living room, letting in warm sunlight that brightened the hardwood floors. As I walked toward the front of the house again, the early-morning sun moved upward in the sky It fell across my shoulders and made its way to the opposite wall, where my white sofa had sat only an hour before. In front of it, red, green, yellow, and black blocks of color were embedded in the Kilim carpet I'd purchased in Egypt. The room had been an eclectic mix of modern art and artifacts. Now—without furnishings, without modern art, without artifacts—it seemed so much smaller.

Walking into the sun room, I stopped at the windows to look outside again. The light bouncing off the panes flooded my eyes so I could barely make out the van. I moved into the shadows; yes, the van was still there, and the boys were drinking coffee from paper cups and smoking cigarettes.

I am not very social; two or three friends are enough for me. I guess you could call me a loner. I think that was why moving to a strange, new place was not off-putting to me. I'd traveled to Europe, Mexico, Central America, and Africa alone, and had been just fine with it. I actually like being by myself; I like challenging myself and being confronted with new situations. It makes me feel stronger.

I remember when I decided to go to Africa, my daughters were concerned.

"But, Mom," my older daughter said, "are you sure you want to go that far away from home all by yourself?"

"I'll be fine, Kylie," I said. "It excites me just to think about it." "But what if something happens?"

"Like what? Something could happen right here in Chicago." I had organized and planned my vacation well—which, to me, was the best way to ensure a safe and happy trip. "I don't see a problem," I said. "I can do what I want, when I want, and with whom I want. And I like traveling alone."

Kylie and I were not very close, so I was somewhat puzzled by her concern. Our relationship had been strained since she was a teenager. She didn't let many people in and that included me, no matter how hard I tried.

So I wasn't afraid of new experiences, or going it alone. But
... what if I hated Kentucky? What if I never saw the few friends
I had again? I'd lived in Chicago for over thirty years. It was my
home. I loved the lake, the incredible restaurants, and all the culture the city had to offer. But I knew I couldn't afford to live there
on my teacher's pension, with very little savings and nothing to
fall back on. I'd thought about it over and over for the last year
while teaching at the University. There was no way around it. I
had to find a cheaper place to live.

At least I could make a little money as an innkeeper, despite
that the thought of going into business made me really nervous.
Not because I didn't think I could do it—I thought I could do
anything I set my mind to—but because being in business had
never appealed to me. It sounded boring as hell. And I didn't like
focusing on money or numbers; I considered myself more of an
artist type. I liked to create things: music, art, drama, gourmet
food. I'd even taught dance for a while at one point. I'd always
said, "I will never go into business."

But a bed and breakfast was most definitely a business. And
on top of that, there would be a constant train of people in and
out of my home whenever they wanted. What was I thinking?
I would have to talk to them. I hated chatting. The thought of
talking about the weather made me shudder. I'd much rather
discuss why Chopin's etudes contained such broad, arpeggiated
chords.

It was hard to believe I had lived in Chicago for thirty years.
I'd done a lot in those thirty years—gotten divorced three times,
earned degrees in education and music, taught high school,
worked on a PhD, and traveled in and out of the country many
times. I'd been thirty-four when I moved there, and now, at sixty-four, I was about to start a new career, one I knew absolutely
nothing about.

I must be nuts, I thought, *starting a new business at age sixty-four in a town where I only know one person.* I stood there for a

moment, staring at the empty room. My resolve returned. Yes, it would be an adjustment, but I'd gotten through my divorces and the death of my beloved grandmother, and once the grieving was over, I'd felt emotionally stronger.

I turned and walked through the French doors into what had originally been my dining room. It made a perfect, airy office with lots of space for a huge desk, file cabinet, and my computer. It was in that very room that I'd first started writing my dissertation.

My one-year sabbatical had begun in September of 1992—almost three years earlier. That fall, I'd registered at the University to work on an advanced degree. Since the Board of Education required a complete physical every few years, I made an appointment at my clinic to do it before classes started. A couple of days after my appointment, the clinic called saying they'd found something suspicious on my mammogram. They suggested a biopsy. I put it off until October, and finally went in as an outpatient on my birthday.

The results were not good: I was told I needed a lumpectomy and probably radiation and chemo. I had breast cancer.

I did not quit school and go into cancer treatment hibernation. I continued as planned. Every day for eight weeks, I went to the Michael Reese Cancer Center for radiation in the early morning, took classes at the university in the afternoon, and worked as a teaching assistant in the evenings. I spent most of my recuperation period alone. Although Kylie had taken me to the hospital for my biopsy and lumpectomy, she did not offer to help in any way afterward, nor did she call to see how I was doing. Thank God for Kristie, her sister, who called and e-mailed on a regular basis and let me know how concerned she was. She even offered to make the trip from Austin, Texas, where she lived, to Chicago to be with me a while. But, as usual, I preferred to handle the situation alone.

The radiation was scary to me, so I got through the fear and anger by drawing pictures of "The Radiation Team from Hell."

They sat hunched over on motorcycles, wearing helmets and goggles and looking fierce as they came toward me . . . dead on. I pasted the pictures on the wall over my desk and talked to them disparagingly every day—a trick I learned reading how psychotherapists treated people who were having panic attacks. Somehow, this defused their power over me.

Fortunately, my cancer was only stage one, and they got it all with a lumpectomy and removal of lymph nodes. I hadn't needed chemo.

When the fall semester was over, I treated myself to a summer in Africa. It was very expensive, but I've never regretted it. It took me away from the angst of a year of studying, teaching, and cancer. And it helped with the depression that came once that year ended and my mental state plunged. I went on safari, gorilla trekking, and sightseeing from Kenya to Tanzania, Lake Kivu, Zaire, and Rwanda . . . an exhilarating and exciting trip.

Over that summer, my state of mind gradually stabilized; the trip had done the trick. When I returned to Chicago, I'd been ready for another year of teaching choral music and Chaucer to high school kids. I was so glad to get back to teaching; I missed it and the students.

I finished checking the apartment for things the movers might have left behind and looked out the window again. This time they were gone—on their way to Louisville, Kentucky. I hated to leave this place but decided I'd better get on the road. It was a five- or six-hour drive straight down I-65 to get there, and I wanted to arrive before dark.

I would be staying with Maggie until my furniture arrived from Chicago. We'd met when we were both teaching high school in Chicago. We were good friends. At least, I thought so.

As I pulled away from the curb, I started thinking about how Maggie and I had first met. We were both teaching at the same high school in Chicago. She was in the English department, I was in Music. One of the things that brought us together was our love for traveling. We went on many trips together over the years, from camping in Wisconsin to hostelling through Europe. Another bonding thing was the fact that we were both pretty opinionated, outspoken and eccentric. She was more so than I, but I was frequently sympathetic to her many causes.

Despite having these things in common, our personalities conflicted at times. But that didn't stop us from being friends—although I must say that we each had our own idea of what a friend was. I saw her as a sister and thought of us as being close, or even, as some might say, best friends. But she had never had a sister so I don't think she knew what that was all about, as I was reminded over and over through the years. I wanted more out of the relationship than she did in terms of declaration of feelings, loyalty, and caring. I always felt like something was missing. I guess you could say that I wanted to be closer to her and share personal feelings. But Maggie wasn't much for spilling her guts to anyone, not even a close girlfriend.

The first inkling that this was the case was when I moved to Louisville. She was living two blocks from where I finally settled, in Old Louisville. In fact, she helped me find my house. She'd come with me to check out a historic mansion for sale near her.

As we stood beneath the chandelier in the parlor trying to figure out what in the world I would do with five bedrooms if I bought it, Maggie came up with the solution: turn it into a bed and breakfast. "Oh, that'd be fun," I'd said, not having the slightest notion of what bed and breakfasts were all about, and never having thought of them as *businesses* requiring a specific skill set. To me, they were just fun places to spend the weekend.

Maggie's solution had been a good option, and to my way of thinking, I could learn the business on the job. She certainly had been a big help to me in that situation, but in others, she was a total disaster. Our relationship constantly vacillated between hot and cold. And when it was cold, it was very cold.

Aside from giving me phone numbers for plumbers, maintenance people and so on, that's about all she did for me . . . unless I asked. Weeks would go by that first year, while I was turning my house into a bed and breakfast, and I would not hear a word from her. She never called to see how I was doing, or ask me over for dinner or socializing, or dropped by, although I encouraged her to do so over and over.

In retrospect, I can remember many times back in Chicago that I was hurt by her inaction. She never gave me a birthday or Christmas gift, although she gave gifts to other people regularly. She did not call me very often, but when I called *her* and asked if she wanted to go out to dinner or to the theater, or to take a trip, most of the time she would say yes. So I was actually getting mixed signals.

One time, I invited a few friends, including Maggie, for dinner. The other girls arrived first and we all sat down to have a glass of my favorite French wine, Pouilly Fuisse. I had chilled it and it was delicious.

"Where's Maggie?" Ellen asked. "Is she coming?"

"Yeah, she'll be here eventually. You know she's always late."

We were all teachers working in the same high school and knew that Maggie had a problem with being on time. She'd gotten low ratings for tardiness from the principal many times. By the time we sat down to have our wine, she was already a half hour late. No phone call . . . nothing. That was par for the course.

"How about another glass of wine, girls?"

"Sure, why not," they all answered in chorus.

As I brought the glasses out on a tray from the kitchen, the doorbell rang.

"That must be her." I set the tray on the coffee table in front of the girls.

"Go ahead, ladies. I'll be right back." I rang the buzzer to my apartment to let her in and stepped out into the hallway. Leaning over the banister, I could hear the heavy door to the building slam shut.

"That you, Maggie?"

"Yeah, it's me. Be right there." No apology for being late. Nothing. Again, par for the course.

"Hey, how are you," I asked.

We hugged and walked inside the apartment.

Maggie called out a generic "Hi girls" from the door, walked into the bedroom, threw her coat across the bed, and wandered into the living room. There was no apology.

"So, ladies, we're having homemade Asian stir-fry this evening," I announced.

"Home-made?" Maggie scowled. "You're kidding. Won't that take forever to make? Why didn't you just buy it at a Chinese takeout?" Maggie didn't cook, so she would never make a home-cooked dinner for friends.

"No, Maggie, it won't take forever," I said. "I do this all the time. Okay girls, go ahead and enjoy the wine. I'm going to start dinner. I'll be right here in the kitchen. Maggie, come on and get a glass of this wonderful wine that Carol brought. It's chilled. Here's a glass; the bottle's in the fridge." Maggie filled her glass and walked back into the living room where the girls were laughing and talking.

Maggie hadn't brought anything. She never did.

I was used to cooking with a wok and had already cut up green pepper, mushrooms and onions. I opened a can of water chestnuts and a can of pineapple chunks and pulled a package of almonds out of the cupboard. I had sliced the chicken into bite-sized pieces and had all the right herbs and spices out on the counter before I poured peanut oil into the wok and turned on the burner.

If you've ever made Chinese food in a wok, you'll know that we used to sauté everything separately at a very high temperature, the vegetables, the meat, the almonds and pineapple, removing each different food group to a plate after it was sautéed. Then we'd scrape the bottom of the wok, leaving all the tasty bits. To that, we'd add rice wine, a thickener, a little water, bullion, and soy sauce. Then add everything we'd just sautéed and let it simmer. Nowadays, it's a little different, not so work-intensive. Most of today's Chinese dishes reflect the Asian Fusion movement. I was doing the old method.

I started the rice and popped the spring rolls in the warming oven. Although I hated to admit it, even to myself, I realized that making everything from scratch was not such a good idea. I had forgotten how long it took, and the smoke from the burning oil was starting to make my eyes smart. It felt like I'd been swimming all day in chlorinated water with my eyes wide open. As I continued sautéing each vegetable and each piece of chicken, a filmy coat of oil formed over my corneas and I could hardly see.

"What's going on in there?" Maggie's voice was high-pitched and bordering on loud." Are we gonna eat anytime soon or not?"

I got a little irritated that she didn't even bother to peek into the kitchen to see how I was doing. I could have been prostrate from all the heat and smoke. I was getting really tired from standing and sautéing. I honestly could have used some help, but not one of the girls came to my rescue. I made excuses for the other girls, who had never been to my house before. But Maggie was supposed to be my best friend.

"Hey Maggie, how about coming and giving me a little help?"

"You know I hate to cook," she yelled from the living room, then huffed her way into the kitchen, with the meanest look on her face. "Nancy, why are you asking me to help? I came over to relax. You shouldn't even be making a Chinese dinner from scratch; it takes way too long; I would have gotten take-out," she said.

We got into an argument over how long it was taking and she left the kitchen. I continued to get the dinner together, set the table, and served it within a half hour. The food was delicious and everybody loved it. After dinner, Carol, Ellen, and Lois helped me clean up, then left. When Maggie left, it was in a huff. I reacted by not calling her and she did the same. We didn't speak for a couple of years. Then one day, I got a note from her saying she wanted to be friends again. At first I balked, but then I acquiesced and our weird friendship started up again.

Chicken Stir-Fry (new and easier method)
(Serves 4-5)

Ingredients
1 ½ cups uncooked instant brown rice
Water (see rice package)
1 lb.chicken breasts cut into thin bite-size strips
2 tablespoons vegetable oil
2 cups sliced fresh mushrooms
1 medium onion, cut into thin wedges
1 cup fresh snow pea pods
1 small can sliced water chestnuts
1/2 teaspoon garlic powder
1 tablespoon stir-fry sauce
1 cup chicken bouillon or broth
3-4 teaspoons cornstarch
2 tablespoons sliced almonds, if desired

Instructions
In 1-quart saucepan, cook rice in water as directed on package, omitting butter.

Meanwhile, add 2 tablespoons vegetable oil to a 12-inch iron skillet.Sauté chickens 3-4 minutes and remove from pan.

Add mushrooms and onion; sprinkle with garlic powder. Cook over high heat 4 minutes, stirring frequently. Add pea pods and water chestnuts to pan and continue cooking 2 more minutes.

Mix cornstarch with chicken bouillon and stir-fry sauce. Add to chicken mixture and heat to boiling. Cook over high heat 5 to 7 minutes, stirring occasionally, until pea pods are crisp-tender.

Serve chicken mixture over rice; sprinkle with almonds.

Chapter 2

MAGGIE

When I pulled up to Maggie's front door, hoping that staying with her wouldn't be a mistake, it was almost six o'clock. I had driven straight through without stopping, so I was starving when I walked up and rang the bell.

"Hi, stranger," Maggie said and pushed the door open wide. She was wearing red, her favorite color. Her hair, dyed a light golden brown, was cropped very short.

"I like your haircut," I said, distracted by the huge silver and turquoise earrings that dangled from her ears.

"Thanks. How was the drive down?"Her shirt was tucked neatly inside her khaki pants and cinched at the waist with a leopard belt. She wore expensive-looking sequined flats that glided over her oriental rugs. Taller and thinner than me, she had the build of a teenage boy.

"Pretty uneventful," I said, giving her a hug. "How about some dinner? I'm starving."

"Can't it wait a little while? I'm right in the middle of writing a couple of letters." I had just driven over 300 miles, but as always, what she was into came first. Nothing had changed.

Her newest painting acquisition caught my attention when I set my heavy bags down. She'd been an interior decorator and was very much into art and design. Her home, a Victorian mansion similar to the one I had purchased, was decorated with lots of color, in a unique and flamboyant way.

My eyes were fixed on the painting. I didn't like it at all. It was a huge, maybe five-foot-by-five-foot painting of a nude five-year-old running through a field of flowers. A nude child? On the wall? I found it offensive. And the colors—lots of red, bright yellow, green, and blue—completely dominated the space where it hung. But then, Maggie's style, both decorating and dressing, was always way over the top. She loved grabbing everyone's attention. Her jewelry was always oversized, and her clothing was as bright and shiny as possible—just the opposite of me. I avoided attracting attention to myself.

I lugged my suitcase up to the second floor and deposited it in the little room at the top of the stairs where I stayed whenever I came to visit. It would be a few days before my furniture arrived, and I had a lot to do.

"Maggie?" I walked into her den, where she sat hunched over a sheet of parchment at a card table, wielding an impressive gold fountain pen. The table was strewn with papers, envelopes and stamps.

Maggie wrote everything by hand. She hated computers, and they weren't too fond of her. She didn't even have one. Actually, back then, all I had was a Steve Jobs Apple gifted to me by my school when I left. It was just a word processor—you couldn't get on the Internet with it. In fact, I'd never even been on the Internet by 1995. It would be a while until I could afford to buy a real PC and learn how to use it.

Maggie kept her eyes on her parchment paper. "What?"

"Thanks for the names of your maintenance man and cleaning girl. They'll both be helping me unpack and setting up my furniture. It should be here by Friday."

Maggie stopped what she was doing and looked up. "So glad we found you a house in record time," she said. "Gotta give you a lot of credit, girl. Coming down here the way you did, not knowing a soul but me, buying a house and starting a business . . . I could never do that. Way too much work. To me, retirement means writing notes to friends and going to the horse track."

That was the biggest difference between Maggie and me. I was a workaholic and she was pretty lazy. We definitely had different body clocks—a real problem when we traveled together. I'd be up at dawn, raring to go, and she'd still be sleeping at lunchtime.

"I love that I did it, Maggie," I said. "I can't wait to be my own boss." We'd both hated having to kowtow to the administration in our high schools when we were teachers. Maggie had always been the first one on the picket line whenever we went on strike. I'd belonged to the union too, but hadn't been nearly as involved or vocal as she was.

I held back from telling her I got a little anxiety every time I thought about having absolutely no business experience, except when I was very young and worked in retail.

Maggie took me to a funny little neighborhood restaurant that night—a hangout for locals, she said. That would soon be me, I thought. It was shaped like the boxcar of a train, painted black, with three steep stairs leading up to the front door. A sign over the door said: GET ON BOARD WITH GOOD EATS.

Inside, there were booths all along the front. We sat in one of them, next to low, wide windows overlooking the street.

I looked over the menu and spotted something I'd never heard of. "What's Burgoo, Maggie?"

"I don't think you'd like it," she said.

"Why not?"

"'Cause they throw just about everything in it they can think of: squirrel, birds, rabbit, all kinds of vegetables. It's like a stew. It's a Kentucky thing."

"Ew," I said, making a face. "Sounds awful."

"Yeah, it's pretty bad," she said. "Why don't you try the Hot Brown?"

"What's that?"

"A hot sandwich with turkey and ham and a cheese sauce over the top."

A short waitress with huge breasts and big blond hair sauntered over and leaned against our table. She kept chomping on a large wad of chewing gum and looking out the window.

"Hey, how ya'll doin' tonight? What can I getcha?"

"I'll have the Hot Brown," Maggie said.

"Me too." I wasn't sure what the Hot Brown was, but I figured if Maggie was willing to eat it, so was I.

We opted for peach cobbler for dessert, which was a lot better than the Hot Brown. After we left the restaurant, Maggie took me for a quick spin around the neighborhood. I was surprised and impressed by all the beautiful nineteenth-century architecture and the huge Victorian mansions. When we got back home, I took a hot shower and fell into bed exhausted.

Recipe

Hot Brown Sandwich

The Louisville Hot Brown was first served at the Brown Hotel, in Louisville, Ky., in the 1930s. Crumbled bacon and a white Cheddar sauce top off this open-face sandwich, which is layered with sliced turkey and tomato. Early versions of this Kentucky original were made with country ham. Below is my version.

Ingredients
½ cup butter
½ cup all-purpose flour
3 cups milk
6 tablespoons grated Parmesan cheese
1 egg, beaten
2 tablespoons heavy cream
Salt and pepper to taste
2 pounds sliced roasted turkey
1 tomato, thinly sliced
8 slices white bread, toasted
¼ cup grated Parmesan cheese
8 slices crispy bacon

Instructions
Melt the butter in a saucepan over medium heat. Stir in flour with a whisk or fork, and continue to cook and stir until it begins to brown slightly. Gradually whisk in the milk so that no lumps form, then bring to a boil, stirring constantly.

Mix in 6 tablespoons of Parmesan cheese and then stir in the beaten egg to thicken. Do not allow the sauce to boil once the egg has been mixed in. Remove from the heat and stir in the cream.

Preheat the oven's broiler. For each hot brown, place two slices of toast into the bottom of an individual-sized casserole dish. Cover with a liberal amount of roasted turkey and tomato slices. Spoon sauce over the top of each one and sprinkle with some of the remaining Parmesan cheese.

Place the dishes under the broiler and cook until the top is speckled brown, about 5 minutes. Remove from the broiler and arrange two slices of bacon in a cross shape on top of each sandwich. Serve immediately.

Chapter 3

MAKING THE MOST OF HISTORY

My furniture arrived a few days later, and I moved most of my Chicago living room and a new bed into the huge two-room suite off the middle of the long hallway on the second floor in my new house.

It was February when I bought the house, but I'd waited until school was out in June to move to Louisville. I'd traveled back and forth between the two cities during that time, looking for stuff to buy for the inn whenever I was in Louisville—everything from mattresses, bed frames, and linens to towels, china, and antique silverware. I owned a few antiques, two matching sofas, end tables, and a couple of area rugs. The rest I'd have to buy.

I decided the room across the front of the house on the second floor would be my temporary office and workout room. It was part of a suite, so the adjoining room could be my bedroom. I would eventually have to move to one of the other three bedrooms. There was one more on the second floor and two on the third. I knew the suite would be a good moneymaker, so I would take a smaller room, one that didn't have an *en suite* bathroom (making it hard to sell). Americans have to have their private baths.

Louis, Maggie's maintenance man, put my bed together, and I practiced making French corners with a set of new sheets all afternoon. The draperies the previous owner had left in what would be my bedroom weren't too bad-looking. But the ones left in the front room were the weirdest-looking things I'd ever seen. They had a khaki background with vertical, military-blue stripes from top to bottom—and in between each pair of stripes were little red dancing tulips. I guessed they were supposed to be Austrian curtains, but what they looked like were puffy clown costumes hanging upside-down over each of the floor-to-ceiling windows.

The rest of the house was empty. For days and nights I sat on the hardwood floor in the parlor, leaning against the cold, white plastered walls, trying to make decisions about paint colors, furniture, and décor. Whatever I did, it had to be Victorian, in keeping with the house's architecture and the neighborhood. Old Louisville had row upon row of nineteenth-century homes filled with stained glass, Art Deco fireplaces, crystal chandeliers, winding staircases, and floors made of beautiful hardwoods.

Blue and white would be my color scheme on the first floor, I decided, with accents of rose, burgundy, green, and gold. I custom-ordered blue moiré draperies with ball fringe down the sides and Austrian valances—very Victorian. Then I bought two beautiful deep-blue oriental rugs decorated with accents of rose and burgundy. When the draperies and carpets arrived, Louis put them in place. After that, he hung elegant blue and white French toile wallpaper in the dining room, over which I had him put up prints of French Impressionists in elaborate gilded frames all through the parlor and dining room . ..Monet, Renoir, Degas, Manet, Morisot, and Cassatt. It looked magnificent.

Occasionally, while I was working in my empty mansion, the floors would creak or the house would settle, making me feel a little uneasy. And at times I felt alone and isolated. Maggie rarely called, and I ended up eating by myself night after night, scooting a metal chair I found in the pantry up to a rickety old card table. Each time I dragged it across the tile floor, the scraping sound echoed through the empty kitchen. It was a constant reminder that I was eating dinner alone again. I was baffled by the fact that Maggie, knowing I was sitting in my house alone each night, never even called or stopped by. At times, old angers would fill my head—as they did one particular night when I remembered a trip we took to Europe together.

We had rented a car and driven from Amsterdam to Chamonix in France. We looped around through the south of France and drove back to Normandy. The trip was going well until Maggie got irritated at something I said about her abominable driving, at which point she jumped out of the car, left it in the middle of the street, and walked away.

We were in Dieppe, France, staying at a hostel. I took over the car, found a restaurant, and had dinner alone. The next morning we left for Carcassonne, and we didn't speak to each other the whole time we were there. Sightseeing together was quiet and uncomfortable . . . and definitely not fun.

Strangely, we always managed to come out of these situations still friends of a sort, and we continued going on trips together: to Europe, Canada, Mexico, and destinations within the US. But despite all our traveling together, the friendship had never really been satisfying for me. Why did I stay in it? Two of the major reasons were that we were both single and able to get away any time we wanted, so I always had a traveling buddy, and that, for the most part, we liked to do the same things. But Maggie was never particularly supportive of me and my needs and endeavors, and our personalities were like night and day.

Although we were both creative and sensitive, unlike Maggie, I wore my heart on my sleeve, and liked to analyze everything and talk about feelings, behavior, and relationships. I was pretty uninhibited and somewhat impulsive, while she was a little uptight, and concerned more with appearances. Her head was filled with strong messages her mother had ingrained in her about proper decorum, manners, language, and how to live her life. She had trouble expressing feelings and kept everything inside—the opposite of me. She was also always late, whereas I was always on time; she forgot birthdays, which I never did; and she rarely, if ever, did anything special for anyone—and if she did, it was as an afterthought. While I would try to think of things to give her that I knew she would like, she would give me a T-shirt she'd gotten in return for donating to a festival or something. It wouldn't even be the right size.

Eerie sounds echoing up and down the house's long staircases shook me out of my thoughts. The third floor, forty stairs up, empty and dark, made me think of the forbidden area at Thornfield Manor in Bronte's *Jane Eyre*.

I finally discovered that most of those sounds came from outside. The houses on my block were built close together and straight up, allowing sounds to travel upward so you could hear nearly every conversation on the street—and making it sound like people were inside my house, talking and walking up and down the wooden staircases. It sometimes caused my mind to play tricks on me. *Maybe they're hiding in the closets on the third floor?* I wondered. I was so affected by this that I didn't go near those closets for weeks.

I continued shopping for the things I needed in order to open the doors of my inn by February. I shopped nearly every day. I'd always had the attitude that money was for spending. If I needed anything, I would buy it. And I needed everything: When I began running out of cash, I turned to my unused credit cards, which sat cloistered in my wallet. I tried to resist, but eventually I gave in and happily handed over one of my cards to just about anyone who would take it.

I soon began to meet with other local innkeepers. There were only three others at first, but within a week Donna, an innkeeper from Alaska, joined us and we started having regular get-togethers. She and her husband had just opened an inn three blocks from me. We hit it off immediately, and became fast friends and shopping buddies. Donna had been an innkeeper for several years before coming to Louisville. She knew the value of the Internet for marketing, and she encouraged me to buy a new PC and learn how to use it.

Kylie, who had majored in marketing at Columbia College in Chicago, told me I also needed to learn how to market my inn.

"Why do I have to do that?" I asked.

"Mom, how are people going to know you're there?"

"I'm in the phone book."

"That's not enough. You need a website and brochures. You need to get your name out there."

I knew she knew what she was talking about. But I resisted."Oh my God, Kylie, why do I have to do all that? What about LBBA? Can't they help me?"(Our small innkeeper group had become The Louisville Bed and Breakfast Association [LBBA].)

"Yeah, if they knew something about it. But from what you've told me they don't know much more than you do. You said only one other innkeeper had a computer. Doris, right?"

"Right."Doris was another innkeeper who had agreed to be my mentor. She was the only one who'd been in the innkeeping business over a year. Bed and breakfasts were new to Louisville. In fact, they were really beginning to catch on all over the US at that time.

"Well, talk to her about it and find out what she does to advertise her inn."

I knew marketing my inn was important, and I did get some tips on how to approach it from both Doris and Donna, but I also needed to finish decorating and furnishing my inn, especially the kitchen.. . no small task. That week, the health department contacted me to let me know I'd have to take a ten-hour course in kitchen management, so there was that, too. I was beginning to see there was a lot more to this inn-keeping thing than I first thought.

Since I knew they served Burgoo, a stew-like dish indigenous to Kentucky, at Churchill Downs during the Kentucky Derby, I thought I ought to learn more about it so if guests asked I could tell them what it was. There seemed to be a wide variety of ways to make it. After looking at several recipes, along with some historical information, this is what I came up with.

Made in giant iron pots, it's supposed to cook for twenty-four hours before being served. Early pioneers made a hunter's stew that consisted of whatever choice pieces of meat, from freshly killed game, were available. The meat, deer, elk, bear, or wild turkey was cooked in an open kettle over a fire. Dried sage and pepper were added to give the stew an English flavor.

Later, Kentuckians who had adopted the early pioneer recipe made the stew with deer, rabbit, squirrel, possum or meat from various birds. Restaurants would eventually add leftover meat, such as pork, beef or lamb. There are many jokes in Kentucky about collecting road kill as a meat for making Burgoo. Today, it remains a hodgepodge of ingredients such as chicken, beef, pork, and vegetables, and is served at the Kentucky Derby from massive iron pots with crackers.

No one seems to know the origin of the word Burgoo. It is said that it may be a mispronunciation of the word barbecue, or of the words bird stew. Some believe the word originated in the seventeenth century on the high sea, where sailors subsisted on oatmeal like porridge made from bulgur, the Middle Eastern grain. Nevertheless, it appears to remain a mystery.

Kentucky Burgoo
(serves 6-10)

Don't worry if you don't have squirrel, venison and pheasant on hand. The only true rule in burgoo seems to be that you need at least three different meats, so let your imagination wander. Chicken is obvious, as is pork. But lamb, rabbit, hare, other game birds, duck, muskrat, whatever—it'll all get hammered into submission in this stew regardless.

Ingredients
3 tablespoons vegetable oil
1 to 2 squirrels or rabbits, cut into serving pieces
2 to 3 pounds venison, cut into large pieces (3 to 4 inches wide)
3 to 5 pheasant legs/thighs (bone-in)
1 green pepper, chopped
1 large onion, chopped
2 carrots, chopped
2 celery ribs, chopped
5 garlic cloves, chopped
1 quart pheasant or chicken stock
1 quart beef or game stock
1 28-ounce can crushed tomatoes
2 large potatoes
1 bag of frozen corn (about a pound)
1 bag of frozen lima beans (about 14 ounces) or canned
  black-eyed peas
Salt and pepper
¼ cup Worcestershire sauce
Tabasco or other hot sauce on the side

Instructions

Pour the oil into a large Dutch oven or soup pot and set the heat to medium-high. Working in batches, brown all the meats. Do not crowd the pan or the meat will not brown well. Salt the meat as it cooks. As they brown, move the various meats to a bowl.

Add the onions, carrots, celery and green pepper to the pot and turn the heat to high. Cook the vegetables until they are well browned; you might need to add a little more oil to the pot. When the vegetables have browned, add the garlic and cook for 1 minute. Add back the meats, along with the chicken and beef broths and the tomatoes. Stir to combine and add salt to taste. Bring to a simmer, cover, reduce the heat and simmer gently for 2 hours.

Fish out the meat pieces. Strip the pheasant and squirrel off the bone. Tear the large pieces of venison into bite-sized pieces. (The reason you did not do this right at the start is because venison will stay moister when it cooks in larger pieces.) Return all the meat to the pot and return the stew to a simmer.

Peel and cut the potatoes into chunks about the same size as the meat pieces. Add them to the stew and simmer until they are tender. Add the Worcestershire sauce, mix well and taste for salt. Add more Worcestershire sauce to taste if needed.

Finally, add the corn and lima beans. Mix well and cook for at least 10 minutes, or longer if you'd like. Serve with cornbread and a bottle of hot sauce on the side.

Chapter 4

LIVING IN LOUISVILLE

A t the time I moved to Old Louisville, the neighborhood was still in transition and there was a lot of rehabbing going on. The streets and even the sidewalks were frequently littered, and unsavory-looking characters lurked around every corner—homeless people and drug addicts, as well as an occasional prostitute or two. I wasn't aware of the problem when I bought my house. But when I began to notice, I thought it strange that neither my agent nor Maggie had clued me in. It pissed me off a bit, but I didn't think it would hurt my business. Besides, I really couldn't afford anything on a better street, and I had lived near and taught in the inner city of Chicago for years, so I wasn't too put off by the seamy side of life and the vagaries of the city. I intended to make the best of it.

The first night I spent in my own house, however, I could hardly sleep. The house faced a wide street, and cars zoomed up and down the road well past midnight. I kept dozing off but would awaken every couple of hours, jump up, and peer out the window to try and figure out who was making all the noise. My bed was right next to a floor-to-ceiling window, and all the sounds from the street traveled straight up to the second floor, making it seem like there was a whole crowd of people having a party in my bedroom.

The second night, I was awakened by a woman screaming. I jumped up, climbed over the bed to the window, and lifted the shade. A man with a shotgun was running down the middle of the street chasing a barefoot young girl in a very short red silk skirt and black halter. She was screaming at the top of her lungs.

"Whore! Get the hell outa here," he yelled. "I'm not paying you a damned cent. Get outa here or I'll blow your f***in' brains out."

I jumped back into bed, grabbed the phone, and dialed 911.

"Louisville Police Department. What is your emergency?"

"I think someone's trying to kill someone in front of my house."

"What is your address, ma'am?"

"1213 South First Street."

"An officer will be right there."

I watched from the window as the police car pulled up around ten minutes later. Of course, the two causing the ruckus were gone by then. Who knows what happened to the poor girl. The shotgun slinger could have killed her by that time. The police car rolled slowly down the street and disappeared.

The next morning, determined to walk over to the police station five blocks away, I got up early and went down to the kitchen to make coffee and get the paper. I wanted to check out the headlines for gunned-down females. I sat down out on the deck to drink my coffee and read.

Within minutes, a woman's head started bobbing around in the window next door. It was Sally, whom I'd recently met while emptying my garbage can at the alley. What a mouth she had on her. I couldn't tell if all the yelling she did was at her dogs or her husband. I was used to foul language from teaching high school in Chicago, but this was above and beyond anything I'd ever heard.

"These dogs have shit all over the kitchen," I heard her scream.

"Well, clean it up, stupid," a male voice roared back at her.

I could hear every word they were saying. It went on and on. I jumped up and went back into the kitchen to call Doris.

"Doris, what's with all these degenerates in Old Louisville? How am I supposed to open a bed and breakfast here? Who would ever want to stay here?"

"I don't know. You should have thought of that before you bought the place."

I was a little taken aback by her response, but actually, it was right in keeping with her modus operandi and personality. Doris was the no-nonsense, officious type . . .very serious about her business. She'd been running her inn—an eleven-room B&B two streets over from me—for a while, and had a business and marketing background. She looked like the caretaker of a girls' school in her old-lady lace-up shoes, white starched sailor blouses, and overly long skirts. And to top off the whole look, her hair was tied in a knot at the nape of her neck. She was a little scary, and I certainly wouldn't have wanted to cross her.

With all this in mind, I just thought my complaints, rather than voicing them aloud: *Oh swell, that's a big help. Thanks, Doris. Why should you care? You're on Third Street, the nicest street in Old Louisville.* The rehabbing had been going street by street, from West to East, and was just getting to mine.

"Why don't you try calling your alderman?" Doris suggested.

Yeah, right after I shut Sally up and stop by the police station.

When I hung up, I called Donna to see how she was coping with the neighborhood.

"Not so good," she said.

"So, what are we gonna do about it?" I asked.

"We? What do you mean, we?"

"We can't just do nothing; we're locals now. Old Louisville is our neighborhood. And we have businesses here," I said, settling into the wooden chair next to my kitchen desk.

"There's not much we can do by ourselves," Donna said.

"I know." I thought about all the other people in the neighborhood. There must be some who felt the same way we did and wanted to do something about it.

"You think maybe we ought to join one of those neighborhood associations?" Donna asked. "I heard there's one for every block. I know there's one for my street."

"And one over here called the Toonerville Association," I said.

"Toonerville? Why do they call it Toonerville?"

"There used to be a train called the Toonerville Trolley that went up and down on the next street over. The association includes my street and the next two east of me."

"Isn't there a meeting place in Central Park called The Old Louisville Visitors Center where residents get together to discuss neighborhood problems too?" Donna asked.

"I think so," I said. "What do you know about it?"

"They're supposed to be working on getting rid of all the prostitutes," Donna said.

"Good idea," I said. The previous night's sinister street dance flashed before my eyes. "Speaking of prostitutes, have you seen any over your way?" I walked out of the kitchen into the parlor and took a quick look out the front window.

"Every now and then," she said. "Actually, I see one sitting on the curb across the street right now . . . wait a minute."

"Donna?" I could hear Donna though her phone as she walked across the hardwood floor of her living room and pulled open the old squeaky front door to her inn.

"On your way, honey, unless you want me to call the police."

"That's better," she said. "Another prostitute has moved on. Now if we only we could get rid of the slum landlords as easily."

"Like the one next door to me?" I pictured Sally's head bobbing up and down in the next-door window that morning. The building was probably Section 8. I'd never seen a landlord there.

"I heard they're trying to change the zoning so the houses that are turned back into single-family homes can never be reverted to apartments again," she said.

After telling Donna about the last two nights, and about Sally, I called my alderman. I found out that inspectors gave out fines for litter and not cutting the front yard grass. Right then and there, I decided I'd call every inspector I'd met and every agency I could think of in Old Louisville until I got some results.

Old Louisville had seemed tame to me when I still lived in Chicago and was coming down only on weekends. With its tree-lined streets and beautiful historic mansions, it had seemed like a virtual Camelot. I'd had no idea when I bought my house that the neighborhood still had a long way to go before it became regentrified. *Darn Maggie. She should have warned me.* I didn't blame my realtor; she, after all, had been trying to make a sale. But here I was, stuck with something I'd never had to deal with before. There were definitely areas like this in Chicago, but I had never lived in one.

During that first year or so, I saw a lot of positive changes take place in the neighborhood. Many of the houses were snapped up at a good price and turned back into single-family homes. Donna and I joined our neighborhood associations, and got together for lunch often to compare notes. We were serious about our businesses and knew we had to get behind local organizations to support change.

I've included this recipe in remembrance of the day I tried relaxing with a cup of wonderful Columbian and French Roast on my back deck, only to be disturbed by the swearing and cursing of my next door neighbor whose voice accosted me through her window.

Recipe

A Great Cup of Coffee

My next door neighbor continued to ruin my morning coffee break on my back deck until she moved. I love coffee, strong and black. I grind my own beans so I can get just the right flavor. My favorite coffees are Jamaican Blue Mountain and Kona, but we don't use them in the bed and breakfast because they're way too expensive. We use a nice European blend and mix it with French roast at the bed and breakfast, which gives it a little bite. All our brewed coffee is made with freshly ground beans. It makes a huge difference to the taste. The most common method of brewing coffee in America is the drip method. No matter which method you use, the following tips will apply:

- Always use fresh water.
- Use 2 tablespoons of ground coffee of your choice (except for espresso) to every 6 ounces of water.
- Always use the proper grind for the equipment you're using.
- If using a manual device, use water that is just under the boiling point.
- Serve coffee immediately after making. Don't reheat coffee. Don't reuse coffee grounds.
- Clean your equipment regularly.
- Never leave your coffee on the burner for more than twenty minutes.

Chapter 5

A NEW WAY OF LIFE

The Third Avenue Café was just a block from Donna, so we met there often. The food was good, and they had decent selection of wines. It was one of only five good locally-owned restaurants in the area, as far as I was concerned. Ermine's, down at the corner of my street, was a wonderful deli and bakery. Amici's was a quaint little Italian place with great pasta and pizza. Buck's, in the Mayflower Hotel, served great, eclectic American food, with impeccable service and an inviting atmosphere. Finally, there was 610 Magnolia, very expensive but amazing. Everything else was fast food.

Buck's was my favorite. When you entered the door you stepped inside a dimly lit reception room where, stretching from the door to the open dining room, there was an elegant mahogany bar. Bent-wood stools with burgundy velvet seats were lined up along the front. In back was a mirrored wall reflecting multicolored bottles of liquor and whisky. Literally hundreds of white Star of Bethlehem flowers in crystal vases were everywhere—on the bar, the ebony grand piano, and the dining room tables. This was the place you took your wife or partner to on your anniversary. I loved it, and I knew my guests would too.

610 Magnolia, also fabulous, was hidden away on a side street. I recommended it occasionally, but it was very pricey. Reservations needed to be made weeks ahead, and it was definitely for serious and adventurous foodies who wanted to indulge in an expensive three- or four-course, rotating prixfixe menu with wine pairings. The proprietor, Chef Edward Lee, who would later do a stint on *Top Chef*, created amazing dishes.

The leaves began to turn and were starting to fall from the trees. Indian summer smiled down on Old Louisville and warmed the tables and chairs of the Third Avenue Café. Donna and I sat outside at a little round table under the trees by the side of the building. She had brought Sophie, her English sheepdog, who lay next to her the whole time. People in Louisville loved dogs. All of the outdoor restaurants welcomed them, and even set out bowls of water for them. I had been dying to tell Donna I'd bought a dog.

"You did?" she said.

"Yeah, a golden retriever . . . named her Samantha. She's adorable, three months old. I'm taking her to doggie training camp today. She'll stay there two weeks."

"Two weeks? She's just a puppy."

"I know, Donna, but I won't have time to train her while I'm running the B&B." I was opening my inn in a couple of months. I really thought a dog would add to the whole ambience of the bed and breakfast, especially if she were well-trained. Besides, I missed not having a dog, and I knew a golden would be wonderful company. "I've heard good things about this place," I told her, "and it looks great. After they train her, we go back twice a week and train together. It'll be fine."

I could tell Donna thought the puppy was too young for an overnight training camp, but I'd already decided to do it.

"How are things going down at your B&B?" I asked, trying to change the subject.

"Really good," she said. "Going to a neighborhood meeting tonight. I learned a lot at the last one." She held her wine glass up so the waiter could see it was empty.

"Like what?"

"Well, our association is in charge of the St. James Art Show."

"You're kidding? That's the show that raises thousands of dollars for Old Louisville, right?"

"Yeah, it's the first weekend in October."

"Isn't it the third largest art show in the nation?"

"That's what they say."

We ordered our favorite Greek salads and crusty garlic bread. I skipped the wine this time—didn't want to chance getting a migraine, something I'd had to worry about since I was twenty-one. I had just gotten married at the time, and had recently started a new job for General Motors at one of their plants. I took over the management of the testing department after they'd had a huge explosion in the plant. The offices were nearly destroyed, so they had to move all the office employees into a couple of metal hangars where they built airplanes. Everyone was under stress. No one had an office, the hangar was dirty, dusty, and hot, and some of the departments were actually disbanded.

We punched in very early each day, and would all go out to lunch together in groups when it came time for a break. Our group found a local hangout with decent food and a bar, and we downed Bacardi cocktails by the pitcher full to bolster ourselves so we could go back to the chaos that was our workplace. The cocktails allowed us to finish the day, a little tipsy but smiling.

Although my headaches had started before that job, they got worse with all the alcohol, dust, dirt, and hot weather. In retrospect, I think being married was also stressful for me. I was used to being on my own and doing what I pleased, and was not good at checking everything out with a partner.

So when Donna ordered another glass of Chablis, I abstained, and spent the next fifteen minutes listening to her talk about her unhappy marriage, with me playing marriage counselor. Although I was no longer married, it was a role I assumed often with girlfriends. I liked to listen, and they liked to complain. After one of these gabfests, I was always happy I had lived alone for years.

That year I had my first Christmas in Louisville. Both my daughters and their families came to spend a few days and check out my fourteen-foot Christmas tree. I invited Maggie and her daughter as well, despite the fact that they'd known I was alone at Thanksgiving and still hadn't invited me to join them. Donna had come through, though, and I'd joined her and her family for a turkey dinner.

Maggie handed me a small package wrapped in wrinkled pink tissue paper on Christmas Eve. I opened it and saw that it was a T-shirt she'd won in a summer festival the year before. I'd gotten her a membership to one of Louisville's wonderful art museums, but she didn't seem embarrassed by the comparison.

The neighborhood was looking up a little by this point. The police had just about rid the streets of prostitutes after receiving continual pressure from all the neighborhood associations, the mayor, and our aldermen, who had finally come through with support and funds.

Despite the recent improvements in my neighborhood, I was still concerned about the building on the corner nearest me, where a string of restaurants kept going in and out of business. Recently, the building had been leased by a thirty-something female lawyer who'd turned it into a health food store. I'd been so pre-occupied getting ready to open my inn I hadn't had time to check out the status of the new store, so I gave Maggie a call to find out if she knew anything. She always seemed to know what was going on in Old Louisville.

It was nearly February, and I hadn't talked to Maggie in several weeks, but it wasn't bothering me as much anymore because of my relationship with Donna, as well as the other friends I'd met at neighborhood and bed and breakfast association meetings. Besides, not being a very social person, I preferred spending most of my time alone, psyching myself up for the torrents of guests who would soon be knocking on my door.

When I finally called Maggie, the first thing I asked her was if she'd checked out the new health food store.

"No," she said. "Did you forget I'm not a health food nut like you are?"

"Yeah, I guess I did for a minute." So like Maggie to give me a smart-ass answer.

"How's the business going?" she asked.

If she really wants to know, why hasn't she called in weeks? I thought. What I said was, "I'm opening the tenth of February. What's going on with you?"

"Well, when you called I was taking a look at some of the horses that may run in the Derby."

Maggie was totally ignoring what I'd just said about the opening of my bed and breakfast. She wanted to talk about the horses. She was really into horse racing. Not as much as her mother had been, but enough to have yearly passes to Churchill Downs, attend the Derby, and spend at least five or six days a month at the track.

"Are you going to the Derby this year?" I asked.

"Don't know yet. But even if I don't, I'll watch it on TV and place a few bets."

"How do you even know who to bet on?"

"I try to handicap the race."

"What does that mean?"

"Well, you find out as much information you can about the horses, and then you pick the one that has the best markers."

"What kind of markers?"

"Things like how many races he's won this year, how many times he came in second or third, who his parents were, who's the trainer, and so on. There's a whole passel of things you look at."

"Then what?"

"You bet."

"How much?"

"That depends. Why don't you come with me to the track when it opens in a few months? You'll catch on in no time. I've got two passes. We can have lunch and stay all day."

Surprised at the invitation, I accepted.

I looked forward to the spring meet in May. I had only been to a horse race once in my life, but now I lived in Louisville, Kentucky, the home of Churchill Downs and the Kentucky Derby. I didn't know it at the time, but I would soon learn to love it, and Maggie and I would eventually make going to the track a regular thing. It took me a while, but I did finally catch on to the handicapping thing, just as she said I would. I never really got hooked on the gambling part of it. I just loved watching those beautiful horses run.

Maggie and I spent a lot of time together once the track opened in May. It never ceased to amaze me how our relationship would be going in one direction, then suddenly turn around and head the opposite way. I thought about it a lot. It had bothered me for years, but now it was starting to make me angry. I couldn't figure it out. The only thing I knew for sure was that it could spiral down at any time with seemingly no provocation. And when we weren't seeing or talking to each other for weeks at a time, that momentum wouldn't change unless I called her. It was never the other way around.When I did call, she would always say yes to almost anything I suggested—dinner, a movie, the track, whatever.

I found that very baffling, and somewhat unsettling. I never accepted the fact that she rarely initiated our doing anything together. And I don't think I ever really forgave her for not being more supportive those first couple of months after I moved to Louisville. To me, friendship was a two-way street—but Maggie didn't seem to see it that way.

The lunches and occasional wine-sipping get-togethers were some of the best times Donna and I spent together. Although I rarely overdid it with the drinking, I frequently cooked with wine. We served this recipe for breakfast as our fruit item. My guests loved it.

Pears in White Zinfandel
(8 servings)

Ingredients
8 pears
2 cups white zinfandel
2 tablespoons lemon juice
1 cup sugar
2 teaspoon cinnamon
zest of 1 lemon
1 teaspoon vanilla
Crème Fraîche
Mint leaves

Instructions
Peel pears and then core from the bottom up, leaving the stems intact. Set aside. In a deep saucepan, combine wine, lemon juice, sugar, cinnamon, lemon zest, and vanilla extract. Bring to a boil. Add the pears with stems up, and scoop spoonfuls of liquid over them. Simmer until pears are tender, 10 to 20 minutes. Remove pears and place in individual serving dishes. Strain liquid and boil until reduced by half. Pour wine sauce over pears and let cool. Serve with crème fraîche on the side and garnish with mint leaves.

* *Crème Fraiche* can be purchased in any gourmet grocery store. Or you can make an easy "mock" version yourself, by combining 1 cup of whipped cream or Cool Whip with 1 cup of sour cream and 2 tablespoons of sugar. Gently fold together. Do not beat. Serve on the side.

Chapter 6

THE MAKING OF AN INNKEEPER

The bite of winter penetrated my feet as I stood on the cold tiles of the bathroom floor. Shaking from the morning chill, I grabbed my long-sleeved Henley shirt from the back of the door, pulled it on over my head, and buttoned it up to the top, then tugged on a pair of corduroys. Winters in Louisville were only ten degrees or so warmer than Chicago, so I was glad I'd brought all of my winter clothes with me. And thank God for mukluks: they locked in the warmth of my heavy woolen socks. I shuffled through the kitchen door and filled the coffee grinder with French Roast. The smell of freshly ground coffee was intoxicating. I picked up my cookbook and thumbed through the pages as Sam, who'd been cuddled next to me all night, jumped down from our roll-away and ran across the cold kitchen floor, her nails clicking against the linoleum.

Heavy thumping reverberated overhead as bright sunlight made its way through the antique glass of the side door and flooded the kitchen. The boys were up! It was time to begin cooking my first breakfast as a city-certified, honest-to God innkeeper. I had to focus. I'd never done this before, and didn't really know where to start.

The night before, ten healthy-looking farmers had checked into my inn. I'd felt a little overwhelmed as they marched into my small Victorian parlor. Ned, the burly leader of the group, stood at least a half foot taller than all the rest, his bushy red hair crying out for a good haircut and some styling. His checked shirt and carefully pressed overalls gave him away.

"I'm a dairy farmer, missus," he announced. "We all come down from Wisconsin to give your Farm Machinery Show the once-over." He thrust a huge hand forward and smiled broadly. "This here is Charlie. This is Al and James . . ." He went on down the line until he'd introduced every last one of them.

"Well," I said, "I imagine you boys are tired after such a long drive. I'll take you up to your rooms so you can get a good night's sleep." I grabbed five keys from the reception desk and started up the stairs. They groaned with the weight of each of the men. "There are snacks and drinks in the dining room. Just help yourselves," I told them, then deposited two in each of the five guest rooms, being sure to tell them all about locking the front door when they went out, and about coming down to breakfast at the appointed time.

Now it was morning, and my house echoed with the sound of boots on my hardwood floors overhead. Soon my weekend visitors would enter my dining room, ravenous and ready for breakfast. I was on my own this week, without an assistant or any help, while the Farm Machinery Trade Show, which brought 40,000 farmers to Louisville, was in full swing.

I had had no idea what the Farm Machinery Show was, or that Louisville was fifth in the United States for conferences and trade shows, until very recently—but with the help of a couple of the local inn keepers I'd befriended, I managed to fill up my guest rooms and open my doors on time. In an effort to recoup some of the money I'd spent on startup, I'd decided to rent out all five bedrooms, including my own, and sleep on a rollaway in the little hall outside the kitchen. The rollaway wasn't too comfortable, but I'd fallen asleep happy, thinking about all the money I'd make that weekend.

I was far more concerned about the fact that I knew nothing about running a bed and breakfast and had no business experience than I was with the fact that I was sleeping in a hallway. The whole thing was totally new to me. *But,* I kept thinking, *how hard can it be? I'll just learn on the job.*

I pushed the thermostat up to sixty-eight and turned on the oven. Warm air permeated the room, and the heady smell of French Roast energized me as I tied the strings of a freshly laundered apron around my waist. I carried a pot of fresh coffee and a pot of hot water into the dining room and placed them on the hot plate, next to the blue-and-white Meissen coffee mugs.

The thought that I'd never worked in a restaurant or hotel and had never prepared a breakfast for paying guests, never mind ten of them, made me nervous, and I wasn't sure my plans were on track. I wanted my first breakfast to be flawless. I was a good cook, but I'd lived alone for years and ate mostly Cheerios for breakfast, which hadn't exactly prepared me for gourmet mornings. So I'd called Doris the night before for help with the menu. I told her I'd decided on a sausage ring, scrambled eggs, Grand Marnier French toast, a fruit cup, muffins, toast, orange juice, and coffee and tea.

"Grand Marnier French toast?" Doris asked."What about grits and sausage gravy? They're farmers. And why so much food?"

"Just because they're farmers doesn't mean they won't like gourmet food," I said. I knew Doris was probably right about there being too much food, but I wanted to make sure I had everything covered.

When the oven was hot enough, I put the sausage ring in and started on the rest of breakfast. As soon as it finished baking, I took the ring out of the oven and unmolded it onto a glass cake plate. It sat there looking miserable, all battleship-grey and unappetizing; it needed to be browned. I popped it back in the oven and went out to the dining room to make sure everyone had orange juice and coffee.

The minute I returned to the kitchen, I heard a loud bang in the oven. The cake plate had exploded—and looking through the glass door, I saw that it was melting all over the inside of the oven. *Of course, a cake plate is not meant to be put in the oven,* I chastised myself. When I opened the door, a thick cloud of black smoke gushed into the room, stinging my eyes and forcing me back against the worktable. Grease oozed out all over the floor and the smoke set off the fire alarm.

I ran around the worktable to get a roll of paper towels from the kitchen sink and slid halfway across the room. After grabbing onto the edge of the worktable, I straightened myself up, grabbed the paper towels, and threw large strips all over the greasy floor, then hurried to turn off the screeching smoke alarm. Thank God there was a stone load-bearing wall between the kitchen and dining room. You couldn't hear a thing on the other side of it. I peeked in on my guests to make sure, just as a Vivaldi Concerto Grosso wafted across the room. It was such a lovely picture.

I grabbed a nearby ladder and leaned it against the wall under the alarm, then climbed up to the twelve-foot ceiling and yanked out the batteries. Back in the kitchen, I got some ham from the fridge and started plating the food as fast as I could. Splat! Something cold and wet hit the back of my hand. I looked up and saw water drizzling from the chandelier onto the prep table. It just missed the fruit bowl. *Oh my God!* I thought. *We'll all be electrocuted.*

The water trickled its way across the ceiling from where the bathroom was on the second floor. The drywall bulged downward, about ready to burst. I knew I couldn't do anything about it then. *Just pray hard,* I thought, *and get the food out fast.* I grabbed a bucket and set it on the table to catch the drips and began repeating to myself, *Stay focused and composed. And keep moving!*

I opened the door to the dining room, and for a moment, the fiasco in the kitchen came to a standstill. When I walked in with my tray-load of breakfast food, the boys started clapping and raving about how wonderful everything looked. They were completely unaware of the chaos all around them. As I set each platter of food on the buffet table, they attacked it like crazed animals, brushing me aside to get there first.

I watched as the scrambled eggs disappeared, and the French toast dwindled piece by piece. The two largest men in the group loaded their plates to the whopping brim. Eggs, bacon, ham, French toast, everything they could get their forks into. I kept running back and forth to the kitchen to get more muffins and butter and refill the orange juice and milk pitchers. I managed to make more coffee and slip in a few more pieces of ham amid dangerous stabs of fork tines.

"Ma'am, can I please have another glass of milk?" became the morning mantra. By the time they were finished, the milk was all gone, the orange juice carton was empty, and all of the muffins I'd stayed up making the night before had disappeared. There was not a shred of food left in sight. It was like the locusts had come and gone.

I learned a couple of important lessons that day about letting guests loose to devour the buffet table. It's best to control the food portions by plating everything in the kitchen and serving at the table. And it was a mistake to make so much food. If my guests hadn't been men with large appetites, I would have thrown away half of what I made—and the health department had warned me I couldn't serve leftovers. Tomorrow, it would be biscuits and gravy.

God, I was tired . . . but there was no time to rest. I had to clean everything, and then run to the grocery store for milk and orange juice. I fell into my kitchen desk chair, coffee pot still in hand, trying to erase from my mind the sight of those ten stalwart farmers devouring all that food.

Then I remembered the grease and paper towels all over the floor.

My feet were killing me, and my whole body was aching—but I got up, yanked off my greasy, wet apron, and pulled my shirt off over my head. Sweat was running down the back of my neck, catching strands of my hair and turning them into twisted ribbons of wet licorice. I grabbed a clean shirt out of the dryer, tied on a clean apron, and walked out into the cold air on the deck, where I collapsed onto the chaise lounge and began taking in deep breaths of clean, fresh air, my wet hair cooling my neck as I lay back on the striped canvas. I closed my eyes against the morning sun. The cold air caught my exhaled breaths and turned them into smoky wisps that rose slowly toward the clear blue February sky.

Wow! I thought. *What a morning that was.* And it was only the first one. All I could think of was, how was I ever going to make any money if I kept feeding groups like this one? Breakfast could cost more than the price of a room.

The crisp winter chill urged me off the chaise lounge and back into the warmth of the kitchen. I decided to call Doris to see if she had any suggestions for feeding large groups of farmers. I hoped the next day would be different.

But oh my God, I had forgotten all about the plumber. I needed a plumber. I didn't even know one in Louisville, but I needed to find one before I did anything else. I headed for the phone to call Maggie. She knew everyone in Old Louisville and always got the best deals on everything.

"Maggie, I need a plumber ASAP."

"What happened?"

"I'll explain later."

As I said, Maggie could be a big help at times, especially when it didn't involve emotions. She gave me the numbers of a plumber and a general maintenance man who lived in the neighborhood. After reaching and pleading with the plumber for a few minutes, he finally agreed to come by after breakfast and try to assess the damage.

The plumber arrived just as my guests finished breakfast and took off for the Convention Center. They would be gone for the day. Sam, who was getting used to people coming in and out of her house, made a beeline to the door. The three of us walked into the kitchen together, Sam wagging her tail like this stranger was her best friend. He stood and stared at the ceiling with his hands in his pockets for what seemed like hours, occasionally running his fingers through his hair. There was a slight ringing in my ears, and it was beginning to unnerve me.

"Well?" I asked. "Can you fix it?" The ringing in my ears had gotten louder. I took a deep breath and looked him squarely in the face.

"Sorry to have to tell you this, Ms. Hinchliff, but that's a pretty serious leak," he said.

"How serious?"

"Well, the only way to really know is to tear out part of the wall in the second-floor bathroom."

"Oh my God! Tear out part of the wall? Are you sure? Isn't that a little drastic? There's got to be something else you can do instead."

"No ma'am, that's about the size of it."

My heart was pounding so loudly I could hardly think. I pictured a troop of plumbers, wrenches and axes in hand, smashing the hell out of my bathroom wall—leaving dark, gaping holes that oozed dirty, icy water—and me pleading with them not to leave as they walked off the job. My stomach was doing flip-flops.

"How much will it cost?" I took another deep breath and tried to calm down. All I could think was, *how will I ever pay for this?*

"Well, it all depends on how much damage there is," he said. "The pipes are probably pretty old and rusty. Cracks have most likely formed, and water has started seeping through. We'll have to replace the old pipes with PVC. I think you better do it right away. The water's probably coming down from the second- or third-floor shower or tub. All these pipes are connected, so every time someone uses them, you'll have a problem."

"It'll have to wait until Monday, when my guests check out," I told him. That way I'd have a little time to think about how I was going to pay for the damage, and maybe ask Maggie and Doris for advice.

"Okay," he said. "I can do a temporary, stopgap fix, and if it leaks anymore, you'll just have to put out some pails to catch the water. We'll see you Monday at seven A.M."

"No, not seven," I said. "My guests don't check out until eleven."

"Okay," he said, "see you at eleven fifteen."

The front door slammed shut and I walked back into the kitchen to start cleaning up the mess, thinking about ways to get some extra money. I managed to soak up the rest of the grease in the kitchen with more paper towels and mop the floor. I filled the dishwasher with breakfast dishes, sprayed the inside of the oven with oven cleaner, and wiped off all of the counters and the kitchen table. I had always been good at house cleaning. In fact, I found it therapeutic.

A little more relaxed, I wandered into the parlor and collapsed into a comfortable wingback chair. I thought maybe I could do some catering, or teach school part time—or borrow some money from Maggie: she had come into a huge inheritance when her mother died one year earlier.

I needed to get my wits together and come up with something fast. I've always had the notion I could do just about anything I set my mind to. That may have been in the back of my mind when I decided to open up a bed and breakfast in the first place. But I'd really never wanted to be in business; I'd just wanted this house. I sank back into my wingback and stared at the ceiling. It had been a little over a year since Maggie and I had first stood face-to-face under the original gaslight chandelier that hung overhead. At the time, the house had been empty and for sale.

I remembered asking her if she thought I should buy a place with five bedrooms. "What am I going to do with that many bedrooms?" I'd asked. "I'll be rattling around in the place all by myself. But the house is so amazing . . . a historic mansion . . . and in great condition." I really wanted it, stained glass and all. "A house like this would cost me over a million dollars in Chicago." And the owners were only asking $108,000. That's when Maggie suggested I turn it into a bed and breakfast. Louisville loved bed and breakfasts. The whole town was filled with Victorian mansions, stained glass, and historic charm, including Churchill Downs, the famous racetrack which opened in 1875 and where the well-known Kentucky Derby is held each year.

Sitting there under that same chandelier, exhausted from my first day as an innkeeper, the thought that it had been a great idea seemed to have lost its magic. When she'd suggested it, I'd only hesitated a second or two before gobbling up the idea with relish, but now at this moment I wasn't so sure I'd done the right thing. I'd made a decision that would change my life forever, not taking the time to think it through.

At the time, I knew absolutely nothing about running an inn. And to top it off, I didn't realize I would have to spend every cent I had saved for years, plus my annuity and my severance pay from the Chicago Public School System, to make it work. But, on the other hand, I'd be the owner of a one-hundred-twenty-five-year-old historic mansion in Old Louisville, Kentucky . . .And I'd be my own boss . . . not like when I worked for a huge public school system, being continually pushed around by decision-makers who didn't always have my best interests in mind. I kept vacillating back and forth. *Anyhow,* I thought, *one way or the other, I'm in it for the long run and I'll definitely make it work.*

Recipe

Alek's Raspberry Muffins

In remembrance of all the muffins the hungry farmers consumed that "Opening Day" morning during my first Farm Machinery Show, and the many more we made over the twenty years my inn was in operation, I've included my recipe for *Alek's Raspberry Muffins,* named after my grandson Aleksander.

Ingredients
2 cups all-purpose flour
½ cup sugar
½ teaspoon salt
1 tablespoon baking powder
1 cup milk
¼ cup vegetable oil or melted butter
2 large eggs
1 teaspoon vanilla
1 ½ cups raspberries
Granulated sugar for topping

Instructions
Preheat oven to 425 degrees. Lightly grease the cups of a standard 12-cup muffin pan. Or line the cups with papers, and grease the papers.

Blend together dry ingredients. Add raspberries to dry ingredients and carefully mix just until coated.

Beat liquid ingredients together until light. Pour into the dry ingredients. Take a fork or wire whisk and blend the two gently (to avoid smashing berries).

Fill cups of the muffin pan three-quarters full. Sprinkle with sugar, if desired. Bake muffins for 15 to 20 minutes, or until a toothpick inserted into the middle of one of the center muffins comes out clean. Remove from oven and cool on baking rack.

Chapter 7

WHAT'S FOR BREAKFAST?

When I first opened my bed and breakfast, I made everything from scratch, including granola, muffins, and cinnamon rolls. I even whipped my own fresh cream and made my
own jams and jellies. I'm sort of a purist when it comes to food
and rarely eat anything out of a can except tuna fish. I prefer to
make my own soups and sauces, and I'm very big on fresh fruits
and vegetables and meat and fish from a meat market. I even
prefer to use fresh herbs from pots on my back porch. And, of
course, I grind my own coffee beans.

I guess I was influenced by my mother and grandmother.
Even though we lived in Detroit, a fairly large city, I grew up
during the Second World War and we had an extensive Victory
garden in our backyard where we grew our own fruits and vegetables. What we didn't grow ourselves, we bought at the fruit and
vegetable stands that dotted the dusty country roads of Michigan. I remember taking long, leisurely drives with my family and
returning home with huge baskets of tomatoes, apples, and grapes.

My mother did a lot of canning in the basement. When you
walked down the stairs into the cool, dark concrete, you could see

what looked like giant cocoons of cheesecloth hanging from the ceiling. Underneath each one was a pail into which thick, purple, syrupy stuff dripped for hours. The mingled smells of plum, grape, and blueberry hung in the air like a sugary veil. She made the most delicious jams and jellies. I can still taste those wonderful flavors, sweet and sour at the same time, making my mouth water under my tongue like I'd just eaten a fresh lemon.

Sometimes the smells changed to the more pungent aroma of vinegar and tomatoes, or the sweet comforting fragrance of fall apples as they boiled together in huge metal pots on the stove my daddy moved downstairs and planted against the far wall. Shelves lined the opposite wall as repositories for the rows of canning jars filled with jams, jellies, sauces, and vegetables. They were lined up like soldiers, with fat see-through bellies and metal caps. I've never tasted chili sauce and applesauce like that again.

Our Victory garden had everything imaginable growing in it. In the summer, my sister and I would gather lapfuls of plump, ripe cherry tomatoes and sit in the cool green grass of the backyard with a salt shaker, eating and laughing. It was then that I first developed a love of fresh fruits and vegetables ripened in the summer sun.

Although I had been a "food snob" most of my life, staying a purist was next to impossible when we became really busy at the inn. I just didn't have time to make everything from scratch, or to can, or to make fresh bread and granola every day.

Some of the other innkeepers had started using mixes, precooked bacon, and even precooked omelets. I couldn't bring myself to do the precooked omelet thing, but I did try a few mixes, and started using precooked bacon. I held out to the end on real whipped cream and homemade granola, but eventually gave up on that too. One of our signature dishes was a quiche; it started out as a simple spinach quiche. But one of my favorite assistants was a Culinary Arts student so I trusted her to work with me on developing new recipes. She and I kept adding more to it and tweaking it so it would taste better. Soon it had a blend of herbs and spices, sautéed onions, and mushrooms. Guests constantly told me it was one of the best quiches they'd ever tasted.

Breakfast at my inn moved beyond bacon and eggs, and I continued to collect recipes and to try out interesting gourmet dishes. There was always the aroma of freshly ground and brewed coffee, made from the finest European blends with a dash of French Roast, and homemade muffins, waffles, French toast, and pancakes. All four were favorites with my guests, but they especially liked my German baked-apple pancakes, made with Granny Smith apples.

Although I had to pull back, at times, on the amount of money I spent on food and supplies, I very rarely scrimped on breakfast. I bought the best coffee beans, waffle mix, and fresh fruit. My kitchen assistants (students at the Culinary Arts School at Sullivan University) and I were always coming up with wonderful and unique dishes to serve.

One of my favorite assistants was Alison, a Culinary Arts student. Ali loved to bake and made the most wonderful cookies and muffins. She had been at Sullivan for over a year when I hired her. Most students graduated within a couple of years, but she was double-majoring in Savory and Pastry chefing, which would keep her there closer to three years. I was pretty happy about that, because it meant she'd stay with me a little longer than most students.

One day I told her we were going to develop a new signature quiche using fresh baby spinach, lots of herbs, and mushrooms sautéed in butter. I asked her if she knew how to chiffonade the spinach.

"Of course," she said with a big smile on her face, happy that I'd asked her to use one of her newly learned chefing skills.

The quiche was pretty work-intensive, but well worth the time and effort. When we began perfecting it, the first thing Alison had to do was chiffonade the spinach. She really seemed to enjoy piling the baby spinach leaves one on top of the other, then slicing them into perfect little dark green ribbons. Next came the mushrooms. She was so deft at slicing them, they didn't stand a chance: she placed the heads in a row and sliced several at a time on a cutting board, quickly making uniform pieces that she tossed into a waiting skillet where she'd melted a couple of table-spoonfuls of fresh butter. After that, she cut thin pieces of sweet Vidalia onion, which she threw in on top of the mushrooms. The aroma made my mouth water.

Alison was one of only two assistants who worked for me at the inn that I considered to be real "sous chefs." She said she had learned a lot about cooking and baking from her grandma and felt she knew more than most of the other students in her class at the school on the day she entered. In fact, she said, the majority of students knew nothing about cooking or baking before they signed up for one of the programs. That was a revelation to me, and it explained why so many of my student assistants seemed to know very little about cooking in general.

The first quiche we made was just okay . . . edible, but nothing special. We wanted to develop it into a real gourmet delight, so we headed for the pots of herbs growing on my deck.

We experimented with the herbs for a week or so, testing each quiche on our unsuspecting guests and getting feedback. The feedback was pretty good, but no one was raving yet. I knew something was missing. I had a very well-developed palate, as did Alison, and she agreed that we had to come up with the missing ingredient. We were adding the vegetables and herbs to a mix of three shredded cheeses, pressing it into a pie shell, then pouring a mixture of eggs and half-and-half over it. Along the way, we discovered that adding a half cup of sour cream helped the taste and texture. But still something was missing.

One sunny morning I came rushing into the kitchen.

"Ali, I know what it needs!" I said.

"What? Tell me, I'm dying to know."

"Pizzazz! That's what it needs . . . a good dose of it," I said.

"What do you mean? What kind of pizzazz?" We brainstormed, and came up with adding a little cayenne to the egg mixture and some grated Parmesan and cracked pepper sprinkled over the top. Now, indeed, it had pizzazz. The next day, when we served it to our guests, they unanimously agreed that it was the best quiche they had ever tasted.

Alison's Spinach Quiche

Ingredients
1 cup sliced mushrooms
1 tablespoon olive oil
1 tablespoon butter
1 cup Mozzarella cheese (shredded)
½ cup Mexican cheeses (shredded)
1 cup Swiss cheese (shredded)
1 cup chiffionade of fresh spinach
1 teaspoon basil (dried or fresh, minced)
½ teaspoon dill (dried or fresh, minced)
¼ teaspoon Cayenne pepper
½ teaspoon garlic salt
fresh cracked pepper (to taste)
1 pie crust
5 eggs
1 cup half-and-half
½ cup sour cream
grated parmesan (to taste)

Instructions
Sauté mushrooms in olive oil and butter until browned and slightly crisp. Set aside.

Line a quiche pan with pie crust. Crimp around edges. Combine cheeses, spinach, and seasonings and press into pie shell. Distribute sautéed mushrooms across top of cheese mixture.

Process eggs, half-and-half, and sour cream together in blender until smooth. Pour over cheese mixture. Fill to top. Sprinkle with cracked pepper and grated parmesan. Bake 45-50 minutes at 400 degrees. Top should be lightly browned.

Chapter 8

CULTURALLY DEPRIVED

When I first moved to Louisville, I thought I was going to be culturally deprived. I had moved from Chicago, where there was a fine orchestra and a superb opera company, several dance companies, and many top-notch theaters and museums. All my life I'd been exposed to this type of culture and couldn't imagine living without it. It had become an intellectual and emotional need. But I was wrong about Kentucky, which I'd always viewed as a state lacking in the finer things of life. Right after I moved there, my first experiences were mostly with theater.

"I've got tickets to *Fences*," Maggie said one day, out of the blue. "Wanna go?"

"Of course, are you kidding?" I said. "I haven't seen a play since I've been here."

"Pick you up at seven thirty, then. It's at Actors Theater."

The night of the show, we parked in the theater garage and took the stairs to the second floor (the elevator was jammed). It was my first time there, but Maggie was an old hand at finding her way around. She was a consummate theatergoer, season tickets and all.

"Where are we sitting?" I asked.

"In my regular seats," she said. These, it turned out, were right in the middle, around twenty rows back.

I pulled off my coat, arranged it over the back of my seat, and snuggled back into it to warm myself against the chill of the auditorium. It felt so good to be in a theater again. I loved the familiar velvet draperies on either side of the stage, the low lights, and the faint whispering of the audience, which increased in volume as the auditorium filled. I opened my program and began to scan the cast.

"James Earl Jones is playing the lead tonight?" I whispered, surprised. "I didn't know Louisville got famous actors to come to town."

"Well, who'd you expect," Maggie retorted, "Mr. Green Jeans?"

"No, but . . . "

I should have expected a sarcastic response from Maggie. She was always on the defensive when it came to her beloved hometown. But it seemed we both had somehow gotten in the habit of jabbing back and forth at each other. Nothing too serious. But gradually, since I'd moved to Louisville, something deeper had seemed to develop underneath. It almost felt as if she resented my being there.

From the time I moved to Louisville, my feelings were continually hurt by Maggie. For those first few months, when I was busy decorating and furnishing my inn, I didn't have much time to socialize. The fact that I actually had no friends, other than her, didn't prompt her to reach out to me or introduce me to folks in the neighborhood. That didn't seem to matter to her. Yes, I was very busy, but there were times when I was very lonely. At first I would call her and urge her to meet me for dinner, and she would. But then, when I realized she wasn't reciprocating, I stopped calling her. And if I wasn't initiating contact, I often wouldn't hear from her for weeks.

One summer, after I'd been in Louisville a few years, I invited her to a Victorian garden party my bed and breakfast association was hosting. She was sitting at a table with me and three of my friends (by that time I had developed other friendships), and one of them asked how I happened to move to Louisville. Before I could answer, she popped up with, "Well, it wasn't my idea."

I was embarrassed and humiliated and really hurt at the way she had blurted that out. I was becoming more and more disenchanted with our relationship, and my friends and family were urging me to end it.

Maggie and I were both emotionally sensitive; we had similar intellectual curiosity and abilities; and we both enjoyed all things cultural, historical, and educational. But there were many differences. One was the extent to which we were open about our feelings. I was an open book. Maggie was not. If she hurt my feelings, I was ready to spill my guts, but over the years I'd learned not to go there with her, because it made her uncomfortable. I was introspective; she was focused out on the world. Things and causes were more important to her than the people close to her. I was the opposite.

That Christmas, I bought Maggie a membership to the Speed Art Museum—and I'd bought one for myself, too. The museum was only a few blocks from us, and my thought was that we should continue broadening our cultural horizons. And, of course, that was when our relationship was at its best. Being members of this small, very special museum changed our theater nights into afternoons with nights at the museum. We started attending the weekly events, as well as many of the fascinating exhibits the curator brought to our city.

A couple of months later, I called her up. "Maggie, the Speed Museum has an Impressionist exhibit from Scotland. I absolutely have to go. Wanna go with me?"

"I can't this time, Nancy," she said, "but next time for sure."

Okay, so my theater and museum buddy was flaking out on me. *Well, that's all right,* I thought, *I'll just go it alone.* I had to see the Berthe Morisot paintings. I was a real champion of women, women's issues, and Impressionist painting. Any woman who was able to insinuate herself into the Paris art scene was a woman after my own heart—and soul, too, for that matter. I loved Morisot's work.

I drove up to the museum, parked in their garage, and went in the back door, eager to get inside. There's something about museums; I don't know what it is, but I just love them. I quickened my step as soon as I got through the door.

"Just one, please," I said. The woman behind the counter tore off a ticket from the huge roll that lay curled up next to the cash register."Oh, I almost forgot," I said. "I want one of those tape player and earphone things." I handed my pass over to the docent and found the nearest bench.

When I opened the brochure, there she was in all her glory: Berthe Morisot, wife of Eugène Manet, Eduard Manet's brother. It was a self-portrait. All of them, the Impressionists, would be there today, hanging on the smooth white walls of the museum, ready to leap out at me. I was so excited the butterflies in my stomach were about ready to exit through my mouth.

When I got to the exhibit hall, I struggled to fit the earphones over my head and find the right button on the recorder to begin the tour.

"Excuse me," came a voice from behind me. "Can you move a little to the right, please?"

"Sure," I said, not turning around, and shifted over.

"Nancy?"

I turned and there was my friend Emma and her husband, standing with their brochures in hand and headphones dangling.

"Hey, what're you two doing here?" I asked.

"We're members," Emma said."What a great exhibit. We've seen it once, but decided to go through again. We don't want it to end. How about lunch in the museum café later?"

We ended up seeing the whole exhibit together and having

lunch at the museum restaurant. What a lovely day. Perhaps I
didn't need Maggie quite so badly as I thought.

So far I'd been to the theater, and seen a world-famous art
exhibit. Not bad for a city that I'd thought would have very little
to offer in the way of the art and cultural activities. *What's next?* I
wondered. I was ready for something new.

Since I'd just seen an exhibit of French Impressionists, I thought
something French would be in order for this recipe. I can't remember where I first got the recipe for Grand Marnier French Toast,
but I think it was from a friend of my daughter's. Anyhow, that
was a long time ago and I've changed it many times since then.
It's a favorite of my bed and breakfast guests. Everybody loves it,
including me. It's not exactly low-calorie, but then most bed and
breakfast dishes aren't. But we are capable of cooking low-calorie
dishes and also food for restricted diets, such low-sugar, non-
dairy, or non-gluten diets. It's always a challenge for me when
guests ask for special diet food. I've learned to make wonderful
non-gluten muffins and pancakes, and other items that meet the
needs of special diets. Most stores now carry special flours, milk,
cheeses and other foods for restricted diets.

Just about every bed and breakfast that I know of serves
some kind of French toast. A lot of them do a stuffed or caramelized version. An innkeeper friend of mine does "butterfly"
French toast. She places the toast slices on the plate so that they
form a butterfly and smothers them in lemon curd. She then adds
blueberries for the eyes and other fruits and whipped cream for
decoration.

French toast can be prepared and fried or baked just before
breakfast. Or it can be soaked in an egg mixture and left in the
refrigerator overnight, then fried or baked in the morning. It is
usually served with fruit, maple or fruit syrup, sugar or jam, and,
sometimes, special flavored butters. Ours is soaked in an egg cus-

tard overnight and then baked on buttered pans in the morning. We serve it with real maple syrup and orange butter, which we make ourselves, and bacon or sausage.

Originally, my recipe called for four cups of cream, but I changed it to three cups of cream and one cup of orange juice. It gives it an orangier flavor and cuts down on the cream.

Grand Marnier French Toast

Ingredients

Parisian-style French bread (twelve to sixteen ¾- to
  1-inch slices)
3 cups heavy cream
1 cup orange juice
4 eggs
4 tablespoons sugar
2 tablespoons orange zest
4 tablespoons Grand Marnier liqueur
4 tablespoons melted butter

Instructions

Put 12 to 16 pieces of bread in a large rectangular baking dish.

Mix remaining ingredients and pour over bread.

Put in refrigerator for several hours. Turnover and soak overnight.

The next morning, preheat oven to 350 to 375 degrees.

Brush rimmed cookie sheets generously with melted butter. Lay pieces of French toast onto buttered pans. Brush tops of French toast pieces with melted butter.

Bake for approximately 45 minutes to an hour, turning halfway through baking time.

Orange Butter
Yield: 6-8 servings (serving size: 2 pieces)

Ingredients
6 ounces butter, softened
Juice of 1 orange
Zest of 1 orange
½ cup confectioners' sugar
1 tablespoon Grand Marnier liqueur
Mint leaves for garnish

Instructions
Mix all the ingredients together and form into individual balls or molds. Garnish with mint leaves.

To serve, remove the French toast from pans, transfer to plates, and sprinkle with confectioners' sugar. Garnish and serve two pieces to each person with orange butter and maple syrup.

Chapter 9

IN GOOD HANDS, I THINK

Sitting in the leather chair in his office with a white hand towel clipped around my shoulders, I heard Dr Frazer's voice as he entered the door behind me. "Hi, Nancy. Nice to see you again."

Maggie had referred me to her dentist. He lived in Old Louisville, just a few blocks from me, and was very active in the community. I had met him a couple of times at Old Louisville gatherings and was happy to find out there was a local dentist nearby. He even had a small dental workshop in his garage for emergencies.

Despite the metal and rubber paraphernalia Dr. Frazer moved in and out of my mouth and the scraping of the enamel on my teeth, we were able to have a rather stimulating discussion during my appointment. He was very talkative, and told me all about himself and his interests in Old Louisville. When I found out he liked opera, it opened up a whole new level of conversation. I had gotten a master's degree in Voice at the Chicago Musical College and had studied both Italian Opera and German Lieder.

"I'm on the board of the opera company," he said. "Are you going to see *Turandot*?"

I had seen a lot of opera but never Puccini's *Turandot*.

"I hadn't planned on it. When is the opera season in Louisville, anyhow?"

"It's on now," he said. "You want to go with me?"

I was a little taken aback by Dr. Frazer's sudden invitation. I hardly knew him . . . and besides, he was married.

"When is it?" I asked.

"Friday night, eight o'clock," he said cheerfully. "Pick you up at seven?"

Hey, wait a minute, I thought. *Hold on*. "Can I let you know?" I asked. "I have to make sure no one's checking into my inn that evening first." Besides, I thought, I had to think about this and call Maggie before I could give him an answer.

I found out from Maggie that Dr. Frazer frequently took friends to the opera with him because his wife didn't enjoy it. Maggie had gone with him a few times herself. I called and accepted his invitation.

That Friday night, Dr. Frazer pulled up in an old burgundy-colored Mercedes in pristine condition.

"Great car," I said, climbing up onto the grey velveteen of the passenger seat and turning to face the burled walnut dashboard. The seats were wide and roomy and very comfortable.

"So, are you ready for Puccini?" he asked as we drove away from my inn.

"I'm always ready for Puccini," I said, smiling. I was so excited to be seeing one of the few operas I'd never seen.

We pulled up to the Kentucky Center for the Arts. Dr. Frazer let me out and called out the window, "I'll meet you in the lobby," then pulled away to find parking.

The stairway up to the big glass doors was filled with operagoers as eager as I was to see Puccini's funniest opera. Inside, people were milling around, getting their tickets out of their pockets, and scanning the animated crowd to see if they knew anyone.

Dr. Frazer knew everyone. I soon saw him across the room,

laughing and shaking hands with one person after another. I hesitated to approach him with so many of his obvious fans around him—after all, he was married, and I was sure everyone knew that. But when he saw me, he waved me over.

"Hey, Nancy," he shouted over the crowd, "over here."

I squeezed through two elderly couples and made my way to where he was standing. I was relieved that by the time I got there, he was standing alone.

"Come on," he said, "let's find our seats."

I followed him into the elaborate auditorium, where he handed our tickets to the usher, got a couple of programs, and led me to our seats. We were sitting in the third row center, compliments of the Louisville Opera Board of Directors. The whole time Dr. Frazer was helping me off with my coat, people were tapping him on the shoulder and waving at him.

As soon as the overture began, the room became quiet and the curtain slowly opened. I tilted my head back to get a better view of the stage.

The costumes were outrageous, the sets and scenery amazing, and the singers and actors extraordinary. I was really enjoying the hilarious performance, when I noticed my chair was shaking. I sat there for a moment, hoping upon hope it wasn't an earthquake.

"Sorry," Dr. Frazer said into his handkerchief. He sniffled softly and sat back in his seat.

"What's wrong?" I asked, concerned.

"Nothing," he said, "it's just so beautiful."

I guessed he was referring to the aria the tenor had just finished, because there was absolutely nothing else to cry about. This was one of the funniest operas I'd ever seen. True, there were times when it vacillated between comic relief and death, but not intensely enough to cry. Ping, Pang, and Pong, the three buffoons on stilts dressed in red, yellow, and green clown costumes, were pushing each other around on stage. I could not imagine why he was crying.

Dr. Frazer blew his nose loudly and apologized profusely. I was so distracted by it that I found myself wishing the curtain would come down so I could ask him again about the tears, but I never could bring myself to do it; I didn't want to embarrass him.

"Have you ever tried the white chili at Timothy's?" Dr. Frazer asked me when we left the theater after the show.

Of course I had. Maggie and I frequently went out to dinner together, and one of our favorite restaurants was Timothy's. I'd never had white chili before then, but I soon became addicted to it. Every time we went to Timothy's, that's what I ordered.

"Yes, many times," I said, smiling.

"Want to stop by and have a bowl on the way home?" he asked.

So we went to Timothy's, and I watched Dr. Frazer, no longer crying and sniffling into his handkerchief, gobble up a bowl before I could pick up my soup spoon. Before we left, I got the waiter to give me the recipe. I put it on my blog and in my recipe book. Over the years I made some subtle changes, making the recipe my own. It is so good.

########## *Recipe* ##########

Timothy's White Chili
(serves 6)

Ingredients
2-3 8 oz. cans Great Northern beans
2 lbs. chicken breasts
1 ½ teaspoons oregano
1 tablespoon olive oil
¼ teaspoon ground cloves
2 medium onions, chopped
¼ teaspoon cayenne
4 garlic cloves, minced
6 cups chicken stock or broth
8 oz. chopped mild green chilies
2 teaspoons ground cumin
3 cups Monterey Jack, grated
½ cup sherry
Garnishes: salsa, chopped fresh cilantro, sour cream

Instructions
Sauté chicken in a heavy large saucepan until just tender, about 15 minutes. Drain, cool, remove skin, and cut into cubes.

Heat oil in the same pot over medium-high heat. Add onions and sauté until translucent, about 10 minutes. Stir in garlic, then chilies, cumin, oregano, cloves, and cayenne pepper and sauté 2 minutes.

Add beans and stock and bring to boil. Reduce to a simmer and cook for ½ hour. Add chicken and 1 cup cheese to chili and stir until cheese melts. Continue to simmer for another ½ hour.

Add sherry 5 minutes before the dish has finished cooking. Season to taste with salt and pepper. Ladle chili into bowls. Serve with remaining cheese, sour cream, salsa and cilantro.

Chapter 10

FENCED IN

By spring, I had gotten through the Farm Machinery Show, the Mid-America Trucking Show, and a couple dozen other smaller conferences and trade shows, as well as a few honeymooners, consultants, salesmen, and visiting professors. Winter's devastation glared back at me as I stood on my deck and surveyed the backyard. It looked terrible. I had all but ignored it since I moved into the house.

The owners before me had planted English ivy in both the front and back and just let it spread. In back they'd built areas for growing vegetables by hammering together railroad ties in the shape of rectangles and filling them with planting soil. The veggies had died out and weeds had moved in. I definitely wanted to dismantle all those railroad ties, pull up the ivy, and plant grass.

I thought it might be a good idea to put up a privacy fence, too, since all kinds of people were traipsing though my yard to get to the front. I couldn't let Samantha out there by herself, and I wasn't about to tie her up. At the next neighborhood association meeting, I let everyone know I was looking for someone to put up a fence for me, and someone gave me Rodney's name.

One day Rodney sauntered down to my bed and breakfast and knocked on the door. When I opened it, he was slouching against the white wooden entranceway, looking like a cross between a Hell's Angel and a hard rock musician about to smash his guitar over someone's head.

Rodney was intriguing, especially to the writer in me. And he assured me he knew all about putting up privacy fences. So I decided to hire him—but because of a few unfortunate experiences I'd had with local handymen and contractors, I refused to give him any money up front. I told him we'd have to discuss the project thoroughly before that happened, and asked for a written estimate of the total cost. That was fine with Rodney. He put together a small crew of unseemly rednecks, and they were soon spending their days in my backyard, working on putting up my fence.

A couple of days into the project, I walked out into the backyard and found Rodney planted on the deck in one of my lawn chairs. He was barking orders at his crew, who were scattered all over the backyard, his tattooed arms waving back and forth. A blue-and-white bandana was tied around his head keeping his long hair in place. Steaming ribbons of sweat were running down his tanned forehead and onto his neck, settling into and soaking his Motorcycle Boys T-shirt. He looked at me over the rims of his aviator sunglasses and shielded his eyes from the strong morning sunlight with large, gnarled hands.

"Hi, babe," he said, giving me a nod as he turned his head in my direction.

The strong smell of marijuana nearly overtook me. I retreated, found a chair on the other side of the deck to drag over, and joined him.

"Hi, Rodney. How's everything going?"

"Fine," he said. "The boys are doing great."

I glanced around the yard. The only thing I saw that looked like the beginnings of my privacy fence were ten holes waiting for fence posts. There were five on either side of the yard.

"Rodney, what about along the back?" I asked. "I don't see any holes there."

He guzzled down a whole can of cola, exhaled a loud burp, and rubbed his chest. "You didn't say anything about the back of the fence. We don't have enough slats for that part."

"Well, we'll have to get some more," I said. "I don't want a fence that only goes three fourths of the way around my yard. First of all, the dog could get out—"

"Lady, that was all you asked for," he said.

I was apparently "lady" now instead of "babe."

"Okay, okay," I said. "But I'm telling you now, I'm going to need the fence to go all the way around the yard. Can you do that?"

"I suppose so," he said, "but we'll have to wait until I can get some more money to buy more slats."

Uh-oh, here it comes.

"Don't worry about that," I said, one step ahead. "I'll just put it on my credit card. You and I can go to the lumber yard this afternoon."

That part he didn't like, but he went along with it.

When I went to pick him up at his house—he lived just around the corner—a couple of hours later, there was no sign of him in front, so I walked around back to where he'd said his apartment was. A black skull was painted in the center of the door. I knocked.

The door swung open, and there stood Rodney with a can of beer in one hand, beckoning me to come inside, his hulking frame completely filling the doorway.

When I stepped inside, the rancid smell of pot and alcohol immediately accosted me. Dishes were piled in the sink, and I could see that his bed, pushed against the far wall, hadn't been made in a while, if ever. Several guitars lay around the room, and a double-barreled shotgun hung from one wall. There were books, magazines, and newspapers everywhere, nearly obliterating the dirty carpet. *General Hospital* was playing on the TV, the sound turned down to make way for the loud rock music blasting from a small plastic radio in the opposite corner. A black leather jacket with nail heads melted into the faded flowers of the sofa. I stood there glued to the floor just inside the door.

"Come on in, hon," he said.

I stayed where I was. "You ready to go shopping for wood slats?"

"Yeah," he said, "just let me get my sunglasses."

He apologized for the large pair of blue jeans left in a circle on the floor in front of the door, picked them up, and flung them past *General Hospital,* toward the bathroom at the other end of the room. The door stood wide open, revealing an unappealing toilet, seat up, staring out into the room.

"Sorry, Rodney, but I have someone checking in in a couple of hours, so we have to get this thing done fast," I said. "I'll just wait in the car."

My heart was pounding as I turned, headed straight for my car, and jumped into the front seat. Taking a deep breath, I leaned my head back against the car seat and tried to relax. Just then, I heard a door slam shut, and seconds later Rodney stumbled out from between the bushes at the side of the house. Staggering slightly, he made his way down the path and around to the passenger side of my car.

We drove to the lumber yard and bought some extra slats. It was only after we got back home that I noticed the difference between the new ones and the ones Rodney had purchased: his were rougher and had a lot more knotholes than the ones I'd picked out. They were obviously inferior and cheaper. But by that time I didn't care. I just wanted to get the damn thing done.

The next evening, Rodney's crew left after sticking the posts in the holes. I went out to take a look when they were gone, and found thick, gravelly cement oozing out from everywhere.

Well, it wasn't going to be the best-looking fence in the world. But it was all I could afford—and I would soon be getting rid of Rodney and his boys. In the end, it turned out okay and Sam was delighted that she now had a back yard of her own. Rodney's price had been reasonable, and while it's no beauty, the fence is still standing.

Recipe

Sweet Potato Fries

While his team was working on the fence, Rodney happened to pass by the kitchen door while looking for a shady spot on the deck in which to plunk himself down. The kitchen door was open and he could smell the sweet potato fries we were making for dinner. I saw him peering through the screen and asked if he liked sweet potato fries. He let me know in no uncertain terms that they were his favorites. I'll never forget how he kept peering through the screen, trying to get a good look at them.

Ingredients
1 sweet potato per person
Light olive oil or organic canola oil, as needed
ground cumin
thyme
black pepper
red pepper
cinnamon
For serving: sea salt, Champagne or rice vinegar

Instructions
Preheat the oven to 450 degrees.

Peel the sweet potatoes and cut them into long, thin shoestrings. Toss them into a bowl and drizzle with light olive oil, stirring lightly to coat. Generously season them.

My seasoning mix is equal shakes of: cumin, thyme and black pepper, and a little bit of hot red pepper and cinnamon.

Throw them on a baking sheet. Spread evenly, in one layer if possible. Bake in the upper portion of your oven for about 20 to 30 minutes, until they are tender and sizzling and crispy around the edges.

Season with sea salt immediately. (Adding salt after they roast keeps them crisper.) Serve with a sprinkle of Champagne vinegar (at the table) or scarf them down plain.

Chapter 11

HELP

By the time Derby 1999 arrived, the yard was looking good, Louisville was starting to feel like home, and most of the prostitutes were gone. Sally from next door had moved, and I'd hired a gardener to sod the backyard and plant a few flowers. He filled large pots on the deck with annuals and herbs, and I bought a couple of outdoor tables with umbrellas and a potting bench.

We served mint juleps out on the deck in the late-afternoon sunshine the day our Derby guests arrived. I had picked my horse and was ready to place my bet on the Run for the Roses. I was actually starting to feel like an honest-to-goodness Louisvillian.

I got through the Derby without any help, but by the time it was over, I knew I had to hire someone. The inn was busy all the time now; I couldn't keep doing everything on my own.

I found my first assistant on the streets of Old Louisville. She was loading up her car in front of one of the beautiful old Victorian houses a couple streets over from me. I almost drove right past, but when I noticed her cleaning supplies, I slammed on the brakes just in time to catch her before she drove away.

"Excuse me," I yelled from window of my car. She was busy putting her supplies her trunk and didn't hear me.

"Excuse me!" I yelled again. She turned, hesitated a minute, then walked over to my window.

"I noticed you putting away your cleaning supplies," I said. "Do you do housekeeping?"

She flashed a broad, friendly smile. "Yes, ma'am."

"Are you working full-time?"

"No, just whenever I can pick up a few days here and there."

"Would you be interested in working at a bed and breakfast?"

"I sure would."

I couldn't believe I was interviewing someone right there in the middle of the street. I'd never hired anyone to work in my bed and breakfast before, so I really didn't know what to ask. I pulled the car over to the curb, jumped out, and walked up to her.

She smiled again and held out her hand. "Hi, I'm Margie."

I shook her hand and smiled back. "I'm Nancy. I own the Aleksander House Bed and Breakfast over on First Street, near Oak."

Margie was a tall, healthy-looking redhead with freckles all over her face. Her curly hair was pulled back and fastened at the nape of her neck with a barrette. She was wearing cargo pants, a T-shirt, and a dark blue work apron with pockets all across the front.

"When are you available?" I asked. Again, I had a little trepidation about considering hiring someone off the street, much less even talking to them, but I needed help badly and didn't want to miss this opportunity. Judging from all her cleaning paraphernalia, she had experience. And I certainly didn't want to put an ad in the paper or on Craigslist. You never knew who might come knocking on your door.

"Any time. When do you need someone?"

Never having an assistant before, I had absolutely no idea how many days or hours I would need her. Or, for that matter, how much housekeepers were making in Louisville. I would have to think about what I could afford and check with Doris on the going rate.

"Can you work tomorrow?" I asked. "You can see what the situation is like, and we can discuss days, hours, and salary."

"Sounds good to me," she said. "What time?"

Margie was exceptional at house cleaning, and she even brought her own cleaning supplies, including rags, with her. She knew all about the best cleaning products, how to get spots out of anything, and how to iron. When she showed up at the inn the next day I hired her right on the spot, without further interview or references, although she offered to bring them. And that first year and a half was perfect. For the first time since I'd been in business, I was able to take a few weekends off while Margie inn-sat.

Unfortunately, after that first year and a half, I started noticing some strange, and even erratic, behavior. Margie, who until now had always been relatively easygoing, was suddenly easily irritated, getting mad at the least little thing. She became moody and complained a lot. Then she started showing up late.

One day she asked me for an advance on her salary. She had two little children, so I was glad to help her out. And since she only worked part time for me, I helped her get work at other inns on the days I didn't need her. Despite the change I'd noticed in her I still trusted her completely and continued to leave her alone with the inn from time to time, paying her extra for inn-sitting.

One weekend, I went to Chicago to visit my oldest daughter for three days. A day or two after I returned, I was doing a routine review of my checking account when I noticed I was five hundred dollars short. I went through my checkbook and saw that the very last check was missing.

Margie was the only one with a key to my office. I called my bank and was told that the check had been cashed at a Kroger grocery store near me. The bank sent me a copy, and I saw that Margie had forged my signature. The bank took responsibility and put the five hundred dollars back into my account immediately. Kroger confronted Margie, and she admitted she'd forged the check. Both Kroger and my bank prosecuted her.

Of course, I fired Margie. After a little investigating and a few conversations with her mother, I found out she had been on crack cocaine for months. She had stolen food and other items from two other innkeepers. Eventually, she ended up in jail. It was such a shame; she was a nice girl who, it seems, simply got mixed up with the wrong people. And, even worse, she had two little children.

By the time I fired Margie, my occupancy rate was up to 55 percent and I needed help badly. I limped along without anyone for a while. Occasionally, one of the other innkeepers would lend me their housekeeper for a few hours at a time, but I really needed someone on a regular basis. I sent out e-mails to everyone I knew in search of more help, and finally, after three weeks or so, a friend of mine who lived not far from me called and said she knew someone who was looking for work.

When the doorbell rang, I rushed to open it. A slender young African American man stood on the stoop.

"Hi, I'm Bryan," he said. "Jean Huxley sent me over. She said you might need some help."

"I sure do. Come on in, Bryan. I'm Nancy." I led him into the parlor.

We sat across from each other, him on the settee in front of the windows and me on the blue wingback chair. He was meticulously dressed in pressed blue jeans and a checked cotton shirt. His hair was clipped very short, and his smiling face was a shiny mahogany punctuated with deep dimples. He smiled and relaxed back into his chair. This time, I decided, I would do an interview and ask for references.

"Have you ever worked in a hotel or bed and breakfast before?" I asked.

"I've worked at the Hilton and downtown at the Sealbach Hotel . . . mostly large banquets, waiting tables," he said.

"What about housekeeping?"

"No, but I like to clean. It's therapeutic."

Bryan, it turned out, was a gay ex-ballet dancer. He was also articulate, personable, and friendly. He didn't cook, but he was very helpful with the guests, especially the ones who were "high maintenance," and he could really clean—in fact, he was slightly obsessive-compulsive, and would spend hours cleaning the toilets and polishing up the handles on everything. He loved doing it, and when he was done the bathrooms glistened.

Up to that time, my guests had been pretty ordinary . . . typical travelers looking for a safe, comfortable, and hospitable place to spend a few days. So when other innkeepers told stories at meetings about unusual and even troubling experiences with some of their guests, I often found them hard to believe—that is, until Madame Capriani checked in.

One of the more memorable of my guests, Madame Capriani was an eccentric opera singer who wore the most flamboyant and outlandish costumes I'd ever seen. The day she arrived to stay for an entire week, I opened the door to a woman surrounded by four sturdy gentlemen. My last check-in for that day was supposed to be a single lady only. *Who were all these people?*

"I am Madame Rosalina Capriati," the woman announced, "and these are my suitcases."

I scanned the four men accompanying her and, sure enough, each one was carrying a suitcase. She stood still as one of the men walked around her, through the front door, and to the foot of the stairs, where he planted the suitcase he carried. He then turned toward Madame Capriani and beckoned her inside.

She extended a long, well-rounded arm—covered in red, purple, and green silk with flouncing magenta fringe—in my direction. I stood there speechless as she glided through the doorway, motioning to her other three walking suitcases to follow.

"Excuse me a moment," I said. "Let me get my housekeeper to help you to your room."

I hurried to the kitchen, anxiety wreaking havoc in my stomach. This woman was going to be very high-maintenance. I knew I couldn't handle flamboyant eccentrics on my own. *Thank God Bryan is here to help*, I thought. He had been working for me for a while by this time, and he knew the ropes. Besides, he was pretty eccentric himself, and great with guests who looked like they were going to be quirky and demanding.

Madame Capriani's four groupies left her oversize suitcases for Bryan to carry up to her guestroom and retreated. I never found out who they were, nor did I ever see them again.

As Madame Capriani and Bryan climbed the long staircase together, she gave him a litany of instructions concerning what she would need during her stay. The requests were so over the top I almost choked. I decided to let Bryan be the one to break the news to her that we were running a simple little bed and breakfast in Kentucky, not the New York Hilton; there was no room service, and there was certainly no concierge.

"And when you make my tea," I heard her say, "use a small teapot. Make sure the water is boiling, then put the teabag in first, and let it steep until it's the color of mahogany."

Oh my God . . . good luck, Bryan.

"And just a touch of milk. You do have China teacups and silver spoons, of course? And maybe a little tray? And Bryan, can you bring me an extra pillow? I prefer down."

Each morning before she came down to the dining room, Madame Capriati would rise and sing a couple of choruses of "Musetta's Waltz" from Verdi's *La Traviata*.

She was a little too much drama for me. Every negative thing I knew or had ever heard about artistic personalities and divas applied to her case. First of all, she was almost totally helpless. She would call down to the kitchen and interrupt whatever Bryan was doing. It was always an "emergency."

"Bryan, the TV isn't working right. Can you come up and fix it for me?"

"Bryan, I have no idea how to work the VCR or the DVD players."

"What kind of movies do you have? Can you just sit a while and watch this movie with me?"

Bryan was beside himself. He couldn't get any work done; she kept calling him all day long. She even demanded he be there to help her when she came down each morning for breakfast. She must have thought she was still on stage because, in addition to her colorful costumes, her daily entrances into the dining room were breathtaking.

"Good morning, everyone," she announced one morning, standing at the entrance to the dining room. She always waited for Bryan to lead her to a table. On this day, she wore an emerald-green satin gown, her red curls piled high on her head, her lips ruby red. She looked like one of the bordello dancers in a Toulouse Lautrec painting. When she moved, her long, dangly ear rings jingled in a slow, steady rhythm. Her voice echoed throughout the room, causing everyone to look up.

"Good morning, Madame Capriati." Bryan quickly took her arm and assisted her to her table. She waited for him to pull out her chair, then slowly turned, smiling, and fluttering her eyelashes to the room as she lowered herself forward in what looked like a bow before sliding into her chair. Bryan shook out her napkin and handed it to her with a flair only he could muster.

"May I have a menu, please?" Madame Capriani asked. Of course she knew we didn't have menus; everyone got the same thing for breakfast. But this is the way it started each morning.

"I'm sorry you're saddled with the diva," I said to Bryan after breakfast ,"but you're the one who agreed to be at her beck and call. And good thing 'cause I'm afraid I'd end up insulting her."

"But she wouldn't come back then," he said.

"Exactly," I countered.

A loud crash interrupted our conversation. It came from the direction of Madame Capriati's room.

"Oh my God," I said, shaking my head, "what now?"

Bryan jumped up and flew up the stairs. I just sat in the parlor, waiting for the bad news.

Minutes later, he came back holding the remains of my precious little blue teapot—the one I kept on the shelf in the moon-shaped window next to the registration desk. He set the broken pieces down in front of me.

"Oh no," I said. "How did that happen?"

"She said she was trying to fix the phone and knocked it off the coffee table, along with the teapot."

"What was wrong with the phone?"

"Nothing. It was just unplugged."

"Why?"

"She tried to bring it to the coffee table and it wouldn't reach without unplugging it."

"What? That doesn't make any sense."

"I know. She said she forgot to plug it back in."

"But . . . "

"I know," Bryan shrugged and slapped his forehead with his palms. "How much longer is she staying?"

I sighed. "Three more days."

The phone next to me rang suddenly. I jumped halfway out of my chair.

"Answer that, please, Bryan. It might be her."

He picked up. "Hello. Yes, this is Bryan. Yes, Mrs. Capriati. Yes. The spigot in the shower? Are you in the shower now? No, of course not. You're in your room. In your robe. Yes, of course, I'll run up to your bathroom right now and try to figure out why it's not working."

Bryan handed me the phone.

"She can't figure out how to take a shower."

"Oh, for God's sake." I slammed down the phone. "What is wrong with this woman? I think she just wants attention. No healthy person could be that helpless. She can't do anything for herself."

A loud shriek came from the second floor. Bryan streaked up the stairs again.

In five minutes he was back down in the parlor.

"What the hell happened this time?"

"You won't believe this," he said. "She went back to the bathroom to try the shower again. She climbed into the tub and started yanking on the shower handle, and she pulled so hard it came off in her hand."

Bryan was still trying to catch his breath after his sprint up and down the stairs. "A huge gush of water came out, like out of a fireman's hose," he went on, "and it threw her to the back of the tub, completely engulfing her in cold water." He fell back onto the settee and took a deep breath, trying to suck in the belly laugh that was dying to get out. "When I came into the bathroom, she was flat on her back, still in her robe, gurgling through the heavy stream. She was sopping wet from head to toe."

"Oh my God," I said, barely containing a smile. "Is she all right now?"

Bryan started laughing. He covered his mouth and bent over to squelch the sounds of his laughter. I couldn't help myself. I started laughing too.

"Yeah, she's fine," he managed between chuckles. "Just soaking wet and befuddled."

As the days went by, I retreated further into my own little world and let Bryan take care of the diva. He brought her tea, fixed her TV, and cleaned her room every day. A couple of times I heard her practicing "Musetta's Waltz," but for the most part, she was pretty quiet after almost drowning in the tub.

I hate to say this about a guest, but I was never so happy to see anyone leave in my life.

The longer I was in business, the more I came to depend on Bryan whenever there was a guest who was a little difficult to handle. And as the years went by, there were more than a few. That is not to say there weren't lots of interesting and friendly ones with whom I became very good friends. 30 percent of my business were those repeat customers. But then there was that other 70 percent, of which 10 percent or so turned out to be a little "different", shall we say.

Madame Capriani's Favorite:
Baked Apple Pancake

Ingredients
4 eggs
1 cup flour
1 cup milk
1 stick butter
3-4 Granny Smith apples
½ cups brown sugar
A generous sprinkle of cinnamon

Instructions
Batter: Pre-heat oven to 400 degrees. Process the first three ingredients together in a blender. In a large 3-4 quart wrought-iron frying pan, melt half of the butter. Pour batter into frying pan and set in oven immediately. Bake for 25 minutes, or until lightly browned. While pancake is baking, make glazed apples.

Glazed apples: Peel apples, core and slice as you would for an apple pie. Melt other half of the stick of butter in a sauté pan and add apples. Sauté the apples for two minutes. Add cinnamon and sugar. Continue sautéing until just tender.

When pancake is done, remove from oven and slide onto large serving or dinner plate. Sprinkle generously with powdered sugar. Top with glazed apples. Serve with maple syrup, sausage patties and steaming cups of coffee or ice-cold glasses of milk. Yummm.

Chapter 12

ROBIN

When I opened the door, there she stood next to Donna, feet glued to the azure tiles on my front porch. She looked like a scared little bird—eyes open wide, stringy wisps of hair falling down over her face like wilted feathers. She had no luggage and nothing else but the clothes on her back. She had been staying with Donna at the Rocking Horse Inn and wanted to stay a few more nights, but there was no availability. So Donna asked if I'd be willing to take her in at my place. I was happy to do so, as I had nobody booked until the weekend and needed the money.

Not stopping to chat as she usually did, Donna smiled and quickly ran off to do some errands for the next day's breakfast. Robin walked tentatively into my house.

"Robin, where's your luggage?" I asked.

"I lost it." She looked forelorn and on the verge of tears.

She followed me into the reception room, glanced around, then absentmindedly wandered into the dining room. I went in after her.

"Is this where we have breakfast in the morning?" she asked.

"Yes," I said. "Is there anything you're allergic to?"

"I can eat anything," she said, eyeing the bowl of fruit on the buffet. She was small and very thin, and reminded me of those pictures of starving children from war-torn countries during the Second World War. Her hands shook as she ran them through her stringy hair.

"Where's your jacket?" I asked. It was spring but still a little too chilly to go without a jacket or sweater.

"I don't know," she said. "Can I go to my room now?"

"Sure," I said, and walked her back into the reception area. "I just need your credit card to check you in."

"I don't have one. I only have this." She handed me a Xeroxed piece of paper with a credit card printed on it.

"I used to live in this neighborhood, across the street, when it was unsafe," she said.

"Unsafe? I've been here for years, Robin, and it's always been safe."

"When I lived across the street, I was always scared," she said. "I'm still scared just being here."

That explained the "scared little bird" look and the shaking hands. I asked about the credit card number printed on the piece of paper. She said it was her employer's. He'd faxed her a copy when she was staying at Donna's. She'd lost her card and he was in Germany, so the fastest way to get it to her was to fax it. She gave me his phone number so I could check it out. I called and left a message.

We wandered into the living room and sat down on the sofa, and Robin began telling me about herself.

"I used to work for a modeling agency in New York, but they fired me," she told me. "They're still after me. They want to hurt me."

My eyes widened. "Why do they want to hurt you?"

She jumped up and launched into a different story about why her children had been taken away from her. By this time, I was pretty certain she was paranoid. Whether she was psychotic or just neurotic, I couldn't tell. But she had stayed with Donna for three days with no apparent mishaps, so I figured she was at least halfway sane. I left her in the living room and tried running the credit card number through for a three-day stay. It went through with no problem, so I took her upstairs to her room.

I thought it strange she had no luggage and asked her about it again.

"I don't have any luggage now," she said."I had some but . . . but I left it downtown."

"Downtown where?" I asked. "Maybe we should go get it."

"We can't."

"Why not?"

"Because it's gone."

"Gone? What do you mean it's gone?"

"Well, I had it with me when I stopped at a restaurant to have lunch. . ." She didn't continue.

"Did someone in the restaurant take it?"I asked.

"I don't know. I had it when I came out and decided to go shopping. "

"You went shopping? With your suitcase?"

"No," she said, "I left it on the sidewalk in front of the restaurant."

"Why did you do that?"

"Because I didn't want to carry it while I was shopping. It was too heavy. I don't know what happened to it. It was gone when I got back. I don't know where it went."

She dismissed my reaction, which was one of disbelief, and asked again to see her room. I let it go, figuring I could question her about it again later.

Robin's employer called back later that day, and everything was as she said it was. The days went by, and she never left the house. I put out fruit, cookies, and granola bars every day, as I always do for guests, and at the end of every day they'd all be gone. Tiny as she was, she ate them all up.

She often followed me around, very close to my back, so that if I turned around, she would be right in my face. I mean *right* in my face. I'm a person who likes her space, so I found this more than a little disconcerting.

One day she came down and asked me for candles. I lied and told her I didn't have any. I was afraid she'd burn the house down. The next day, when I went up to clean her room, I discovered she had crept down in the middle of the night, found the candles, gathered up stacks of magazines from all over the house, and brought them all up to her room. Her door was open and she was lying on the bed half naked, magazines strewn everywhere and lit candles sitting all around the room. She had also changed the furniture completely around.

I was appalled at what she was doing and started to say something—but before I could, she asked if she could stay three more nights. I was tempted to say no, but I was short on revenue, so I said okay. I explained to her that she would have to move to another room, though; the room she'd been staying in was rented to someone else for the weekend. Before walking away, I made her promise to keep the door closed.

While I went down to run the credit card through for three more days, Robin decided to take a bath. She only had the clothes on her back, so she'd been washing them every day and hanging them in the bathroom to dry. Despite the conversation we'd just had, she left the bathroom door, which opened onto the hallway, open during her bath, and I could hear her singing clear down on the first floor. I looked up through the staircase just as she streaked across the floor, buck naked, to the linen closet in the hall. She grabbed some extra towels and streaked back to the bathroom, singing the entire way.

I was expecting a houseful of guests to check in later for the weekend. I had been thankful Robin was the only one there for those first three days; her behavior was so bizarre it might have scared anyone else away. Now I thought about the weekend with trepidation. The house would be full, so I knew I had to talk to her about streaking through the hallway, among other things.

The next morning, there were ten for breakfast. Robin came down and acted fairly normal. After breakfast, everyone left for the day except Robin, who went upstairs to take another bath. I went into the kitchen to clean up. When I came back out, I could see and hear her in the parlor, naked again under a half-open robe and bare feet, sitting on the Victorian settee in front of the window and singing "Ave Maria."

I sat down on the settee next to her and explained why she couldn't wander around naked in her robe while there were guests in the house, and that she would have to leave if she continued to do so. She switched the conversation to her boss, whom she said she'd met in Louisville in some bar. He was now her boyfriend, she told me, and lived in Germany but came to the States often on business.

A few days later, Robin announced she would be leaving soon in a limousine.

"Why are you taking a limousine to the airport?" I asked. "It's only five minutes from here."

"Not the Louisville airport, the Cincinnati airport," she said.

"The Cincinnati airport?" I said. "Why go there? That's two hours away."

"Because that's where I came in."

"And you need a limousine to go there?"

I was confused about the whole thing—her going to Cincinnati, the limousine, the quick decision to leave, all of it. Everything about this woman was confusing.

"Well, when are you leaving?" I asked.

"I don't know. Soon."

"Okay." I decided to let it drop and just go with the flow.

The next morning, while I was making omelets in the kitchen, one of my guests came in and said there were two limousines out in front and a driver at the door asking for Karen. When

I asked him if he meant Robin, he said that he was supposed to pick up Karen at this address.

Just at that moment, Robin appeared at the top of the stairs. She had a travel bag strapped over her left shoulder.

"Robin, did you call a limousine?"I called up to her. "There are two of them outside."

"Yes, I'll be right back." She turned and disappeared back up the stairs.

I peeked outside, and sure enough there were two limousines, one white and one black, parked in front of my inn. The two drivers were dressed in black suits and chauffeur's caps. One was standing on my porch, waiting for Karen or Robin or whoever she was. And the other was standing at attention next to the white limousine.

Robin returned without the suitcase. Before she left, I asked her in low voice, "Why did you tell the limousine company your name is Karen?"

She didn't answer; she just kept on walking right out of the house.

I ran her credit card through immediately, and again it went through with no trouble. I was so happy to see her leave I forgot to ask her about the travel bag as she hurried out the door.

There was so much going on that morning, it didn't really register with me that Robin had had a travel bag over one shoulder at the top of the stairs, although she hadn't had one when she checked in. On an unconscious level, my brain had stored that information away, but in the moment I was focused on the two limousines outside, the fact that the chauffeur had asked for Karen and not Robin, the ten paying guests waiting for breakfast, and the half-done omelets in the kitchen. I had to put the whole thing out of my mind and go back into the kitchen to finish up the omelets for my guests.

It was not until a week or so later that I gave it another thought. I was looking for my yoga book, which I'd tucked into one of my travel bags in a hurry and tossed into a closet in one of the guestrooms where I'd spent the night (I still didn't have my own room).I opened the closet door and there, thrown into a corner, was my travel bag. That's when the vision of Robin standing at the top of the stairs with my travel bag strapped over her shoulder flashed before my eyes. It finally dawned on me this was the very same bag. *My* bag.

I opened it and found, crammed into every corner, a selection of my best clothing—clothing that I kept locked in a large storeroom on the third floor in the same room Robin had stayed in. She had apparently found the key and picked out all my best pieces, including a pair of beautiful new leather boots, a linen pantsuit, a cashmere sweater, and other things she could wear in Germany. We were about the same size, so everything I owned would have fit her.

It was a miracle that I had been at the bottom of the stairs the day before when she started down the stairs; otherwise my clothes, along with my dignity, would have been long gone.

Recipe

Yogurt-Berry Parfait
(yield one parfait)

I finally had to stop putting out a bowl of fresh fruit every day. It was costing me too much money. Robin would finish off the whole bowl before the end of the day. I felt a little guilty, though, because I could see how much she loved fruit, so I started including a fruit dish at breakfast. This parfait was one of her favorites.

Ingredients
10 medium-to-large ripe strawberries
½ cup blueberries
½ cup raspberries
Sugar to taste
1 cup vanilla yogurt
1 cup granola
Fresh mint for garnish

Instructions
Slice strawberries into a medium-sized bowl. Add blueberries and raspberries. Sprinkle with sugar and let sit for five minutes, until the sugar melts and berries begin to macerate.

In a large goblet, add ⅓ to ½ of the granola. Tip glass to the side so that granola lies on an angle. Keeping the glass tipped on an angle, layer ⅓ to ½ of the yogurt, then the same amount of berries. Continue layering to the top of the glass. Top with fresh mint.

Chapter 13

THE EXUBERANT HONEYMOONERS

When I looked up the middle of the staircase, I could see Alison leaning over the third floor banister. She was yelling and waving her arms for me to come upstairs.

"Nancy, you've got to see this! You won't believe it."

It was ten o'clock in the morning. Breakfast was over, and all the guests had left for a day of sight-seeing. Alison and I were getting ready to clean the rooms.

"Hurry. You've got to see this!"

I ran up the two flights of stairs and followed her into a room. She stopped and turned to look at me; her hand was over her mouth.

"They trashed it," she finally said. "They completely trashed it."

There were clothes, including Lisa's beautiful white lace wedding dress, everywhere. They were on the floor, the desk, the loveseat, everywhere. There was even a pair of boxer shorts hanging from one of the lamps.

"What's that?" Alison screamed, staring at what looked like a small deflated red balloon. "And there's another one . . . a green one. Oh my God, they're all over the place . . . green, blue, red, and yellow. What are they?"

"Well, what do you think they are, Ali?"

She looked closer, then jumped back. "Oh no. Some of them are full. I'm not touching those," she said. Her whole body convulsed as she ran out into the hallway.

"Ali, we have to. We can't leave the room like this. Run downstairs and get both of us some rubber gloves and lots of paper towels. And a large plastic bag."

Ali came back covered with protective gear: plastic gloves, a long plastic apron, and plastic booties over her shoes. She had secured them with rubber bands. She looked like a workman who had come to fumigate the house—a little comical, but I didn't laugh. She started picking up the prophylactics one by one, holding them up in the air then plopping them into the big trash bag. There must have been close to twelve of them.

"Nancy, the mattress is halfway off the bed and the linens are barely clinging on."

"Where's the mattress cover?" I asked.

"Over there." She pointed to a pile in the corner near the door.

"How the heck did that happen?"

"Look at this!" She held up a huge jar of Vaseline with deep, finger-like gouges in the middle of it. And dropped it the minute she realized what it was.

"Oh no," I said. "Look what they did to Shakespeare!" I had laid a beautiful little book of Shakespeare's sonnets on the table next to the bed. I don't know if they'd read any of it or not, but there was a big red wine stain on Sonnet 18: "Shall I Compare Thee To A Summer's Day?"Dribbles of candle wax were all over the small mahogany table.

Ali was right. The place was certainly trashed.

Lisa and Brian had stayed with us before. Both of them were very young. They'd gotten married the previous day, and last night had been their wedding night. And what a night it must have been.

"I would be so embarrassed to leave my room like this," I told Ali. "Especially knowing that you and I would see all this when we cleaned it."

"I know. I wouldn't have been able to look anyone in the eye at breakfast."

"It didn't seem to bother them though," I said. "They were as happy as clams, laughing at the table and hugging and kissing all through the Belgian waffles and strawberries."

We had been excited about their coming. We felt like we knew them. They were an adorable couple, just barely out of their teens. We wanted their wedding night to be perfect. We'd made their bed with fine white linens and a down comforter. We'd put a vase of roses on the little cocktail table in front of the settee. Next to a bottle of red wine and two crystal wine glasses, we'd set out a fruit tray. I had even gone downtown to Muth's Homemade Candies and purchased some outrageously decadent chocolate truffles.

They had arrived late, and when I took them to their room and they saw what we'd done, Lisa, still in her white wedding dress, was delighted, and Brian had beamed from ear to ear. I'd left them alone and gone downstairs to bed. They wanted a late breakfast, so I knew I would get a little extra sleep that night.

We didn't have this kind of mess to clean up too often, but we managed to clear the room and sanitize it in a hurry. Nothing was really damaged except my beautiful book of sonnets. *Sorry, William*, I thought, *we'll just have to buy another one.*

Belgian Waffles and Fresh Strawberries
(Serves: 2)

The following breakfast dish was an absolute favorite of my guests. When they called to make their reservations, if they had seen it on the bed and breakfast website or if they had been here before, they would ask for it ahead of time. And that's what Lisa and Brian had done. They would have had them every day if we served them that often.

Ingredients
1 cup waffle mix
1 egg
6 ounces water
2 tablespoons butter
Powdered sugar
Strawberries, enough for 1 cup sliced
2 dollops whipped cream

Instructions
Plug in Belgium waffle iron and let heat until ready. Melt butter. Set aside. Combine egg and water. Beat with a whisk. Add waffle mix and butter in small batches, alternating, and beat well until all lumps are gone. Set aside.

Slice strawberries and add 1 rounded teaspoon of sugar. Let set to macerate. Ladle ½ cup waffle batter onto waffle iron and let cook for 3-4 minutes or until golden brown. Repeat.

Remove waffles from iron and sprinkle with powdered sugar. Ladle ½ cup strawberries onto center of each waffle. Top with a dollop of whipped cream and half a strawberry. Serve with maple syrup.

Chapter 14

Another Run for the Roses

We stayed very busy that February through November. It was 2005, and I'd been in business for ten years at this point. I guess I was turning into what you might call a seasoned innkeeper. Unfortunately Sam, my beautiful and very much loved golden retriever had died two years prior. I was so distraught by her early demise that I could not even mention her name without crying. Being busy was a godsend, as I finally learned to live with it.

Spring rolled around again and with it came another Kentucky Derby. I was looking forward to it that year because Jodi and Mike, a couple who had stayed at my inn before, were coming.

The weather played a trick on us that day; the incessant rain stopped suddenly and the sun came out. I sat on the front porch that afternoon, waiting for Jodi and Mike, and enjoying the sweet fragrance of the magnolias now in bloom. It was the last day of April and the crocuses were pushing up through the once wintry ground, softened by the April rains.

Jodi and Mike pulled up in a brand-new Volvo. They got out of the car and lifted their weekend bags from the trunk. Jodi, dressed in jeans and a red T-shirt, removed her cap and sunglasses as she ran up the walk and gave me a big hug.

"It's so good to see you," she said. "You look great."

"So do you," I said. "Will your friends be here soon?"

"I imagine by five. They're driving down together from Okolona."

Jodi and Mike had stayed with me on Derby weekend for the past two years. This would be their third. The first time I met them, they'd ridden down from Michigan on their motorcycles to stay for the weekend. They had met online and decided they'd spend their first night together in my honeymoon suite. They must have had a grand old time in that four-poster bed, 'cause they forgot to close the blinds, and all the neighborhood kids had lined up on the fire escape next door to see the show. My next-door neighbor came running over and nearly knocked my door down trying to tell me someone needed to close the shades.

Mike was a millionaire, though Jodi didn't know it until he asked her to marry him. He had a little plane, and for the past couple of years he had loaded it up with friends and brought them all to the Derby. But this year he and Jodi had a new car, so they'd decided to drive down.

They usually watched the races from the infield, where everyone wore shorts and t-shirts and baseball caps. Neither one wanted to get dressed up, like the movie stars and elite who spent a fortune coming to the Derby every year. It was sort of a status symbol with some. But not with Jodi and Mike; they just liked horses and loved to see those beautiful animals do their thing. You'd never know they were so well-off; they were very laid-back and never flaunted it. I was looking forward to visiting with them before the other guests arrived.

"Mike?" I called. "You gonna make the mint juleps again?"

"You got the fixin's?" he asked.

"Yeah," I said.

"I got it covered," he said, grinning.

When Derby was a week or so away and we'd decided to have our traditional barbeque, Bryan started coming in extra days to get everything done. He polished all the silver, including the huge coffee urn that sat on my grandma's antique walnut chest in the dining room, deep-cleaned the floors, and completely rearranged the dining room, using checkered table cloths for a more casual look. By the time Jodi and Mike got there, Thursday night, we were ready to start the barbecue.

Jodi and Mike's friends, as well as the other guests, would start arriving around four or five; the barbecue would be at seven. This year we were not taking a chance that there would be no rain. Last year and the year before it had rained so hard that we'd had to move everyone inside right in the middle of dinner. We didn't want to go through that again. Sure enough, by four o'clock it was raining like crazy, so we sat in the kitchen trying to figure out how and where to grill the chicken and ribs.

"Should we just grill everything on the deck and keep the lid closed so the food won't get wet?" I asked.

"Or bring the grill into the kitchen?" he countered.

"I'm afraid it would be too dangerous, and the smoke would fill the whole house."

"Oh yeah . . .well, what about just broiling everything in the oven?"

"That'd work, but we wouldn't get that good charcoal flavor," I said.

"I know, but at least we wouldn't get drenched or asphyxiated."

Bryan was right; we had to just transfer all the meat to the oven indoors.

I'd made the potato salad that morning. The baked beans were done and in the warming oven. The garlic bread was ready to pop in the oven, and the blackberry cobbler was baking. We were almost there.

"Bryan," I asked after checking on the cobbler, "have you got everything ready to make the mint juleps?"

"Where's the mint syrup?" he asked.

"In the fridge. If Mike wants to make them, just let him do it. I think he really likes to. Maybe you can just serve them. We'll need the Derby glasses and swizzle sticks, and those Derby cocktail napkins we bought."

Before I moved to Louisville I knew nothing about the Kentucky Derby. I had heard of it, but only remotely. What a surprise it was to find out that it was the biggest event of every year in Louisville, and had been for the past one hundred twenty-five years, by 1995, the first year I was living there. Louisvillians actually started celebrating three weeks before the race ever happened, which was always the first Saturday in May. They hold marathons, balloon races, river boat races, beauty contests, parades, and Thunder Over Louisville, a gigantic fireworks show. Everything is free. The city makes its money from the hotels and restaurants, and Churchill Downs.

In my twenty years in Louisville, I only went to the track one time during the Derby. Maggie had lifetime passes (she inherited from her mother) so we went around back and watched the races from the backside, where the barns are and the horses are kept. We were safely away from the glitz and glamour of fancy Derby hats and mint juleps, which I think are ghastly, and crowds of people. I actually preferred to watch it on TV at home, where I could get a close-up look and concentrate on my horse picks. I've never been a gambler, but I always bet on the Derby. The first year I was there I placed a Superfecta bet, where you pick four horses and if three come in, in any order, you win. I won $300. I kept trying every year after that to win again, but never did.

The Derby is the first leg of the Triple Crown. The other two races are the Preakness, run in Maryland, and the Belmont, run just outside of New York City. The last horse to win all three races was Affirmed, in 1978, until American Pharaoh won in 2015. Several have come close since—the most recent being 2004's

Smarty Jones, a long shot Jodi bet on who won the Derby and the Preakness but missed winning the Belmont by a hair. And there was 2008's Big Brown, who won the Derby and the Preakness but finished the Belmont in last place.

To the locals in Louisville, the Kentucky Derby is much more than just a horse race: it's a social extravaganza and a reason to celebrate. The city bursts with out-of-town visitors and celebrities. Even the Queen of England visited a couple of years back. The men come out in their finest attire, and the women wear their most flamboyant wide-brimmed hats, decorated with everything from flowers to horses.

If you can't afford a box seat or a seat indoors at the Derby, you can buy cheaper tickets for the bleachers or the infield. No need to get dressed up for the infield—shorts and a T-shirt will do. It's usually a pretty rowdy crowd. I've never been there, but I hear there's a lot of beer drinking, yelling, and good old down-home fun. And I've seen it on TV.

Just about everybody in Louisville eats Derby Pie and Burgoo and drinks mint juleps at Derby time. It's a tradition. And in this city of serious traditions, why do anything else? Derby Pie, a chocolate-walnut confection, was first made in Kentucky in the early 1950s by Kern's Kitchen Inc. People have described it as a giant chocolate chip cookie in a pie shell.

Burgoo, the stew Maggie had warned me off trying when I first came to Louisville, used to consist of a combination of small animals like squirrel and rabbit and a variety of birds, with whatever vegetables available thrown in. Today, however, it's made mostly from chicken and beef and has become a tradition at Churchill Downs, as well as many local restaurants.

I don't like bourbon, so you couldn't get me to drink a mint julep if you tried—except maybe if you offered me a lot of money. But I found the history surrounding it fascinating. Early Scotch and Irish settlers in Kentucky brought their whiskey-making skills to America. Since corn was a native crop in Kentucky, these frontier farmers started distilling their surplus corn and producing a new kind of whiskey.

One of the three original counties in Kentucky was Bourbon County, established in 1785. Farmers began shipping their whiskey from the port on the Ohio River in Bourbon County down the Mississippi River to New Orleans. Oak barrels were used as shipping containers. The whiskey aged during shipment and mellowed in the oak wood. The whiskey from Bourbon County continued to grow in popularity.

Like Derby Pie, Burgoo, and Hot Browns, mint juleps have become a tradition in Kentucky—possibly the most famous Kentucky Derby tradition of all. Made of bourbon, sugar syrup, water, lots of ice, and a mint sprig, the mint julep is traditionally served in a very cold silver julep cup. People who go to the Derby drink their juleps out of that year's glass souvenir cup. Today, the Kentucky Derby serves more than 80,000 juleps over the course of the two-day event.

That Derby went on without a hitch. Jodi and Mike's friends were great, and the couple staying in the fourth guest room fit right in. Annie, a friend of Bryan's, came in to help clean up when the party ended, and Bryan got out of the house by ten o'clock. I was exhausted. But at least it was over—that is, until next year.

For five years Jodi and Mike stayed with me on Derby weekend, and Mike always took charge of the mint juleps. Then, one year, they took a cruise instead, and they never came back. That's the way it sometimes happens in a bed and breakfast: one day you're anticipating the arrival of your favorite guests, next day they've dropped out of sight and sound . . . maybe never to be heard of again.

Recipes

Mint Juleps

The proper way to serve a mint julep is in a frozen silver goblet, but you can use glasses instead—just use the most elegant ones you have! You can make the syrup ahead of time and store it in the refrigerator for whenever the julep mood strikes you.

Ingredients
2 cups water
2 cups white sugar
½ cup roughly chopped fresh mint leaves
32 fluid ounces Kentucky bourbon
8 sprigs fresh mint leaves for garnish

Instructions
Combine water, sugar and chopped mint leaves in a small saucepan. Bring to a boil over high heat until the sugar is completely dissolved. Allow syrup to cool, approximately 1 hour. Pour syrup through a strainer to remove mint leaves.

Fill eight cups or frozen goblets with crushed ice and pour 4 ounces of bourbon and ¼ cup mint syrup in each. (Proportions can be adjusted depending on each person's sweet tooth.) Top each cup with a mint sprig and a straw. Trim straws to just barely protrude from the top of the cups. Serve juleps on a silver platter.

Chapter 15

THIS OLD HOUSE

I'd been living in Old Louisville for five years before I learned it was inundated with ghosts. Ghosts that peered from the gardens and leaned against the mansion gates on every block of the area. Ghosts that sat on the steps of the Christian Science Church just three blocks from me. Ghosts that sobbed each night from the windows of the fourth house down on the next street over. They were everywhere . . . so people said. I didn't believe a word of it.

However, locals were convinced that a young girl with black hair haunted my neighborhood. Although she'd died ninety years earlier, she supposedly continued to wait for her betrothed on the steps of the First Church of Christ Science, only three blocks from my bed and breakfast. And on the next street east, there was the "Phantom of Brook Street," a young girl attacked and murdered by two vagrants in the home where she was employed. Although that home had been demolished years earlier, people said her ghost came to work daily. Other ghosts, such as the Widow Hoag and the Ice Boy, had also been seen from time to time, lurking in the shadows.

Old Louisville is the third largest Victorian preservation area in the country. The tree-lined streets are filled with stately turn-of-the-century mansions, built in seven major architectural styles. There are gargoyles, chameleons, serpents, swans, turrets, and towers made of stone, and a variety of wrought-iron fences, hand-carved doors, and stained-glass windows. There are hidden balconies, secluded courtyards, and secret passageways all made from terracotta, glazed brick, tile, marble, and stone. It is one of the most interesting areas in Kentucky.

As David Domine, a Kentucky author, writes in his book *The Ghosts of Old Louisville*, "When the wind picks up and sets the dead leaves on the sidewalk to swirling, you might wonder who lived—and died—in the large brick mansion in front of you. When the air bristles with the fall chill, you could stop and ask yourself why someone is staring down at you from the third-story window of the large, uninhabited gray stone house across the street or why you hear organ music from the abandoned church on the corner."

Mr. Domine's collection of stories centers on the area of Old Louisville where my inn was situated. He refers to the neighborhood as "a Victorian gem forgotten by time that has seen its share of splendor, sorrow and tragedy."

If you've never owned an old house (truly old—one hundred years of age or more), whether haunted or not, in a preservation area, you probably have no idea what it's like. They are beautiful, interesting, and historic, yes. But they also require constant attention and upkeep, as I learned over the years. My inn was an old house, built in 1882. No one really knew who'd done the original work on it, or the rehab, the repairs, and the upgrading, or how well it had been taken care of before I bought it.

The day after Derby ended on my fifth year in the house, I got a taste of the downside of having a one hundred-and-thirty-year-old historic home.

When I first heard the crash that morning, I couldn't imagine what it could be. I was so shaken; I just sat there in front of my computer, fingers still touching the keyboard, afraid to move. After a few seconds, I started obsessing: *Did the bookcase on the second floor fall over? Or that huge mirror over the fireplace in the suite?* There were no sounds of breaking glass, only a very loud thud that shook the whole house. Whatever it was, it had to have been something heavy . . .very heavy.

I jumped up, ran out in the hallway, and started down the forty stairs leading to the first floor. When I reached the bottom of the staircase, a thick black cloud of dust wrapped itself around me. Coughing my way into the parlor, I saw the dust settling on every piece of furniture and the oriental carpet. It had even started making its way into the adjacent dining room. Tangled gray balls floated in the air, and minute particles of debris glistened and danced in the morning sunlight that was streaming through the front windows.

I could see, through the moving veil of debris, dust pouring out of a large four-by-six-foot hole in the ceiling where a chunk of the plaster had fallen to the floor. It's called "collapse" (I later learned), and is common in very old houses. There had probably been warning signs—namely, cracks in the ceiling—before it happened, but I hadn't spent enough time looking up to notice.

The next two weeks were filled with more dust and chaos. We sent the carpets, draperies, and pillows to the cleaners and shoved the furniture from the parlor into the dining room. Repairmen hung huge clear sheets of plastic, in between the parlor and the hallway on one side and the dining room on the other, to keep the dust from the gaping hole and the Plaster of Paris used to repair it from settling all over the rest of the house.

When the ceiling was repaired, crews of workers in white overalls invaded the place with twelve-foot ladders. They leaned the ladders against the walls, covered the floors with paint-spattered drop cloths, and began cleaning everything in sight . . . walls, woodwork, windows, and more. They scattered lunch pails and large empty cardboard cups once filled with Coca

Cola and coffee all over the room. After taking hour-long lunch breaks in the backyard, they returned to work smelling like bologna, corn chips, and cigarette smoke. I tried to focus on the end product, but being such a clean freak and having obsessive-compulsive tendencies, I was in a constant state of anxiety over all the clutter.

At four P.M. sharp each day, the workers rolled up their drop cloths and disappeared. The next day, they returned and continued cleaning the lamps, decorative pieces, and picture frames, polishing the glass of each one and returning it to its proper place on the wall. They vacuumed and shampooed the overstuffed furniture, polished the floor, and again retreated. What an amazing feat. By the time they were done, the house looked better than it had before the ceiling collapsed.

It took two weeks to return everything to order. During that time, we had to close down the inn. Fortunately, I had two insurance policies that covered all the cleaning and repairs. One of them even paid for the loss of revenue during the two weeks we were closed. When the dust blew away, however, so did the policy. I was learning the ropes quickly and would soon be an expert— not only in inn-keeping and maintaining an historic home, but in making sure I didn't file too many claims. And oh . . .remembering to look up and check for cracks in the ceilings.

Anyhow, the whole incident was over now, and I had sparkling clean draperies, furniture, floors, and walls. I'd made a few thousand dollars on bookings I never had, and I had a new ceiling . . . well, part of a ceiling. As far as I was concerned, all was right with the world. At least for the moment.

One night a few months later, I woke with a start to the sound of someone pounding on my front door. I threw my comforter off and jumped out of bed. It was dark and cold as I made my way to the bedroom door and out into the hallway. I stood at the top of the stairs. Moonlight streamed through the transom, lighting a narrow path to the first floor. *Who could be pounding on the door in the middle of the night?* I thought.

Downstairs, I turned the latch, slowly pulled the door open, and peered through the narrow crack. The streetlight shone brightly on the front porch. No one was there. A strong gust of winter wind made its way under the storm door and accosted my already freezing bare feet. The pounding had stopped.

I shut the door, locked it, and turned to climb the stairs back to my room. A sudden loud crack of thunder broke through the silence. The house gave a little groan and swayed as strong winds whistled along one side and icy rain coated the windows. I was alone in the house with the uneasy feeling that always came when Kentucky's winter ice storms returned.

I jumped back into the warmth of my bed and reached over and grabbed the clock from the bedside table. It was 3 A.M. But just as I set the clock back down, the knocking started again— only this time I could tell something, or someone, was knocking on the window. Anxiety started gnawing at my stomach again and I jumped up, ran around to the other side of the bed, and pulled up the window shade. I could hardly see through the glass, which was heavily coated with ice and sleet. As I stood there, something large, thick, and dark came right for me. It hit against the pane right in front of me, swung back, then hit the pane again and again. I finally made out that it was a branch from a tree in my front yard. It was totally encrusted in ice, and was being tossed back and forth by the strong winds.

As the branch moved from one side of the window to the other, it scraped narrow slits of ice away and I could make out the street in the moonlight. Everything was covered in a thick sheet of ice and snow, giving an eerie, dead feeling to the entire block. The only things moving were the tree branches. Many of them ended up crashing to the ground like fallen soldiers.

Suddenly the telephone wires to the south of my house

plunged downward and the street was enveloped in darkness. For a moment, it was like the end of the world.

Oh my God.I wonder if the power is out. I turned around and jumped back into bed, rolling over to the other side. I reached for the lamp and turned the switch. Nothing happened. The clock was dark, so I could no longer tell what time it was. No power. Thank God there were no guests in the house. I lay there listening to the rain pounding against my window and the tree branches swishing as they fell to their icy graves. Since I'd been in Louisville, the winters had brought not only snow and sleet but lots of very strong winds, sometimes with the strength of tornadoes (or even hurricanes), terrible, devastating electrical storms, and heavy rain lasting for days.

Maybe the Ohio Valley had something to do with it, but these storms were really scary. Chicago storms were never that bad. There, I didn't have trees so near the house, so I didn't have branches pounding and scraping against it. And the thunder was never as loud and long-lasting. I don't remember experiencing a blackout in the almost forty years I lived there.

I tried to go to sleep again, but the pounding, scraping, and thudding were too much for me. I finally gave up on sleeping and tried the lamp again. This time it came on, and the clock started flashing. I got up and walked out of the room and down the hall. When I got to the back hall, my feet began slowly sliding towards the linen closet. The whole back hall was covered in water, causing me to almost lose my balance. I managed to slide toward the light switch and flip it on.

Used to glancing up at ceilings now, I saw a familiar sight: a narrow thread of water dripping from a rain-filled bulge in the ceiling. I grabbed a broom from the linen closet in back of me, a pail, and some old bath towels, then glided under the leak and poked a hole in the middle of the swelling to let the accumulated water out. Down came an avalanche of dirty, icy liquid—right on top of me.

Sopping wet, I placed the pail under the leak, threw the towels over the entire back hall, and headed for the bathroom. By that time I needed something to calm my nerves, so I turned on the hot water in the shower and grabbed a robe from the back of the door. I knew there was nothing I could do until the next morning, when I could call Richard.

The shower relaxed me enough to go back to bed, but I tossed and turned the rest of the night. I reached Richard first thing in the morning, before he got out the door. He said he'd come right over if I'd make a pot of strong coffee. Fine with me—I could use a jolt myself.

He was over within minutes. "Why didn't you call me yesterday?" he said, inspecting the damage. "Now you really have a mess here."

"Richard, I didn't even know this happened until three o'clock in the morning. Besides, would you have come out in the horrible storm last night?"

"For you, dear, anything."

Richard was always flirting with me. Although in his early sixties, he was still very cute and had a boyish charm you couldn't resist. He knew the ladies were enamored of him, and made a point of getting a rise out of every one of us. He and I had become good friends over the years. He was the first maintenance man I ever felt I could really trust, and he did beautiful work. He was from North Dakota and had that very strong North Dakota accent—like Frances McDormand's in *Fargo*. He was smart, creative, and very funny. I had a tiny crush on him at one time, even though he was a good fifteen years younger than I was.

"I'll see if I can find where the water is coming in before the next storm," he said, "but it'll take a while."

"Next storm? What next storm?"

"The one that's coming this way from North Dakota." He turned and winked at me.

I didn't know whether to believe him or not. He was always kidding me.

"The dripping water in the second floor back hall is coming from the third floor," he shouted over the banister. He had run up the stairs and was scouting around in the bedrooms.

"From where on the third floor?"

"From the storeroom in guestroom number four."

"Oh, no." That was my most popular room. It was stunningly beautiful, Victorian, with a four-poster bed.

"Yep. I checked it out. It's all wet up here. Those strong winds must have blown in a lot of water. It's all over the storeroom floor. The carpet soaked it up. That's what's causing the dripping from your second floor ceiling."

"Well thank God it's in the storeroom."

"You need to keep a pail under those drips until I can fix it."

"Until you can fix it? I thought you were going to do it today! I'm gonna run out of pails here soon. And old bath towels."

"Can't do it right away," Richard said, coming back down the stairs. "Gotta find out where the water's coming in first. Gotta take a look at the roof. I'll have to wait till the ice clears up. It's too dangerous to go up there right now."

If Richard was saying it was too dangerous, it must be really bad. Being from North Dakota, he was an expert on storms and snow and ice. They usually didn't faze him; he'd gotten so used to them while growing up there. Every time I complained about how cold it was in Louisville, he came back with, "You call this cold?"

I hoped and prayed he would get to the repair before Christmas, as I was going to visit my daughter Kristie in Austin and didn't want to leave the house with a gaping hole in it. But gradually I decided not to worry. I knew Richard would eventually find the leak and fix the problem. He always did.

Ghost in the Graveyard Cocktail

Ingredients
1 scoop vanilla ice cream
2 oz.crème de cacao
2 oz.black vodka
Ground nutmeg, to taste

Instructions
Combine the spirits in a glass and set aside. In a lowball glass add the scoop of ice cream before drizzling the vodka mixture over the top. Sprinkle some nutmeg over the top for garnish.

Chapter 16

NEW YEAR'S EVE

A few months later, there was another explosion. I was getting somewhat used to hearing noises by now, so I didn't pay much attention to this one. There were always strange sounds going on in the house—creaking floors, the house settling, loud trucks and people outside shouting and honking their car horns, fireworks, loud thunder and falling branches from the hundred-and-thirty-year-old walnut tree in the backyard next door.

This time, I was convinced the noise was coming from outside. It was New Year's Eve, and I had returned from Austin just in time to check in two guests and take them to their room on the third floor. They were getting ready to go out to a party when I heard it. It was somewhat muffled, so I decided it couldn't be in the house. And everything seemed to be in place. I checked the bathrooms, the heavy wall mirrors, and so on, all the way down to the first floor. Nothing wrong. Then something told me to take a look in the cellar.

I peeked down the cellar stairs. The entire cobblestone floor was covered in over a foot of water. Horrified, I inched my way down a few more stairs and caught a glimpse of water gushing at breakneck speed out of the side of my water heater.

As I backed up the stairs, I heard one of my guests, Mr. Simpson, coming down from the third floor.

"What's going on?" he asked, spotting me. "We heard this really loud noise and—"

"There's a big hole in the side of my water heater," I said, throwing up my hands. "Water's pouring out all over. I don't know how to stop it."

"Let me see . . ." He took a quick look down the stairs beyond me. "Wait a minute; I'll be right back." He ran upstairs.

I was getting really shaken up by now. I knew I probably wouldn't be able to find a maintenance man on New Year's Eve. But before I could get too worked up, Mr. Simpson came back down from the first floor with rubber galoshes on, ran down the basement stairs two at a time, and walked right into the watery crypt. Within seconds, he found the shut-off valve and stopped the flow dead in its tracks.

I couldn't believe it. Not many guests would have done that.

"I'm so sorry about this. What a way to spend New Year's Eve," I said. "I don't know how to thank you."

"Don't worry about it," he said, "I'm glad I could help. Do you have someone you can call?"

"I hope I do," I said. "I have a list of plumbers in the kitchen. I hate to ruin your evening. Thanks again for all your help. I think I'll be okay now. Let me know if you and your wife would like some hot coffee or tea." I felt terrible about him getting soaked in my basement; I shivered just looking at him.

"I think I'll go upstairs and take a hot shower," he said.

I didn't say anything just then, but I knew he wouldn't be able to take a hot shower. There was no hot water. I would remind him later, after I found a plumber.

As I headed for the phone, Mr. Simpson headed upstairs. At that point, I began to notice it was getting very cold on the first floor. The third floor had separate heating and cooling, so I was pretty sure it was still warm up there—but either way, I didn't have time to think about that. Right now I needed to find someone to come and take a look at the damage as soon as possible. I scoured through my kitchen desk for my list of plumbers, maintenance men, whomever I could find.

I didn't know most of the plumbers on my list, so I called Richard first to get his advice on what to do. He was at a party, but he answered. When I filled him in on the situation, he told me to call the names on the list one by one and call him back if I couldn't find anyone. The first three didn't answer, but the fourth one gave me the number of his cousin, who he thought might consider coming out on a cold, wet New Year's Eve.

"Acme Heating and Cooling," a sleepy voice growled into the phone.

"Tony? I got your number from your cousin, Joey. I have an emergency and Joey said you might be able to help me out."

"What's the problem?" His voice softened a bit, giving me hope that he wouldn't mind getting out of his warm, comfy bed and trekking over the bridge from Indiana to my house in Kentucky.

"My water heater burst wide open," I said. I always exaggerated when I talked maintenance guys, just to make sure they know my problem was serious enough to warrant their attention.

"Did you turn off the water valve?"

"Yes."

"And now the water's receding?"

"Well, no, not exactly."

"No? Is there a drain in your basement?"

"No, there isn't."

"There's no drain?"

"No, Tony, This is an old historic home—one hundred and twenty-five years old. The basement is actually a cellar with bricks on dirt. It's never been finished. It's the same as it was when it was built in 1882. And Tony, it's getting really cold in here."

"Is your furnace in the same area as your hot water heater?"

"Yes, it is, but what has that—"

"Well, all that water probably put out the pilot light."

"Oh no." I sank into the chair next to me. "Is that dangerous?"

"No, it's just damned cold."

"Can you fix it?"

"I'll have to take a look."

After giving Tony directions to my house, I remembered Mr. Simpson upstairs; about to take what he thought would be a nice hot shower. I quickly dialed his room, hoping he hadn't gotten undressed and into the tub by this time.

"Mrs. Simpson? Is your husband there? This is Nancy."

"No, he's in the bathroom about to take a hot shower."

"Oh my gosh, go tell him that we do not have a second hot water heater on the third floor, so there is no hot water. I am so sorry."

I felt bad about my guests being inconvenienced, and was so thankful for their help that I gave them the night free. Eventually we got the furnace turned back on and a new water heater put in—but we had to wait until after New Year's. And it was damned cold the whole time.

I was looking forward to the new year and the warmer weather that would be arriving soon. I had gotten used to thinking about the year in terms of the major events that occurred in Louisville. It would be February soon, and with it came Valentine's Day, the Farm Machinery Show, and a slew of other trade shows and conferences. I'd better start thinking menus and Valentine's decorations and chocolates.

Recipe

A Relaxing Cup of Tea

You'll need a clean kettle and freshly drawn cold water. Warm the pot by swirling a small amount of boiled water in it.

For black tea, only pour on freshly boiled water and do not over-boil it. For green tea, always use the water just at the boil. One teaspoon of loose tea per person and one teaspoon for the pot is about right, but add as much or as little to make it to the strength you like.

Let loose tea brew in a teapot for up to seven minutes. The general rule is: the larger the leaf, the longer the brewing time. Earl Grey and Lady Grey need five minutes, while a smaller leaf tea will only need about four minutes.

If using a teabag, allow it to brew for two and a half to three minutes. This allows the flavor to fully develop. Then add milk or lemon, or enjoy it black, whatever your preference.

Chapter 17

THE NAKED IRISH FARMER

It was February 12th, 2007. Twelve Irish farmers had just filed into my parlor and lined up in front of the stained glass windows. It was the week of the Farm Machinery Show again. There was a leader—a stout, healthy-looking, middle-aged man named Duncan with ruddy skin and a thick Irish brogue.

"Good day, ma'am," he said. "Hope we won't be too much of a bother to ye. We've flown in from Donegal just this mornin' and have come to see the show. Yer place sure is lovely."

"You're all from Donegal?"

"Yes ma'am, Donegal and nearby farm regions. We belong to The Donegal League of Dairy Farmers. We're a-wantin' to check out the latest equipment in dairy farming. And we've brought ye a little present for welcoming us into yer home." He handed me a small square packet wrapped in white tissue paper and tied with an Irish green satin ribbon. "Open it, ma'am. I do think you'll find it quite fittin."

I pulled the ribbon away from the packet. Inside were three beautiful Irish linen dishtowels, one with a colorful map of Ireland printed in the center.

"Thank you . . . all of you," I said. "What a nice thing to do. These are lovely. I will hang them up in the kitchen today."

I took the boys on a little tour of the first floor, the deck, and the garden, making sure they knew that if they wanted to smoke it had to be outside on the deck. Then I showed them to their rooms.

They had booked every one of my guest rooms, so I had to sleep in the hallway outside the kitchen like I had when I first opened. But they were great guys—friendly, lots of fun, and as Irish as they come. That evening, they helped me clear out the small black refrigerator in the dining room by drinking all the leftover beer that had accumulated from other guests. I was grateful for this, because now I was able to fill it with sodas and bottled water.

I dug out my camper cot, set it up, and closed off the six-by-eight space in the back hall. There were seven doors leading into that space: the door to the garden, the basement door, the back stairway to the second-floor door, the door to the kitchen, the bathroom door, the door to the dining room, and the door to the reception area. Those old houses are amazing.

When I went to sleep that night, I closed and locked the doors leading to the dining room and reception area, then fit the bed in between the reception area door and the door leading to the second floor, up the maid's stairway. I clipped a lamp onto a wrought-iron rack of recipe books next to the bed so that I could read myself to sleep, and, since the camper cot was pretty uncomfortable, put a foam rubber pad on it. Even with the pad, a down comforter, and a couple of pillows, however, the cot was still uncomfortable. I was camping in my own back hallway, without the joys of nature.

The door leading to the second floor had pane glass on its

top half, but I hadn't hung curtains on it because no one but me used that back stairway. Besides, when I lay down to sleep, I could see the wall up at the top of the first landing, where I had hung a huge Victorian wreath made of roses and ivy, through the glass. At least it gave me something aesthetically pleasing to look at.

On the second night the Irishmen were at the inn, they returned from the trade show, drank the rest of the beer—which they now stored in the small refrigerators in their rooms—and went to bed. All was quiet when I fell asleep.

I was out like a light when, all of a sudden, I heard a *clump, clump, clump* down the back stairway. It woke me immediately. I looked up to see a completely naked farmer stumbling down the back stairs toward me and my camper cot. There was nothing between him and me except the door to the second floor, and it was unlocked, as always.

I jumped up, bolted for the key and shouted, "Hey! What do you want?"

I guess it scared him, because he turned on a dime and made a beeline back up the stairs, naked rear end and all.

The next morning at breakfast, I heard the group talking about how Terry had been walking in his sleep again the night before. When I came into the dining room, they asked if I'd heard Terry wandering around the house the night before.

"No, I didn't hear a thing," I lied.

My thought at the time was: *I've got to make sure the door to the back stairway remains locked till the trade show is over and the house is empty again;* although, I must admit I rather enjoyed the change of scenery that night on the stairway.

The first night the boys checked into my inn, after giving me my gift, they had asked if I could make southern biscuits and gravy with cheese grits for breakfast one day, a Kentucky favorite. They had read all about Kentucky and were anxious to taste some of our "down home" cuisine. I had obliged, of course, and enjoyed watching the gobble up my cheese grits. The next day, I made pumpkin pancakes and stacked them high on each of their plates, placing a thick chunk of sweet creamery butter on the top of each stack and drizzling them with my homemade maple caramel pecan topping. They were delighted. Everything I made delighted them. They were such a fun group to cook for.

Recipes

Southern Biscuits and Gravy with Cheese Grits
(Serves 10-12)

This version of sausage gravy I made is a beloved Southern recipe—there are many variations to be found, mine being just one of them. Sage and nutmeg are two of the more pronounced flavors in the gravy, giving it a slightly more elevated taste than you would find in simple milk gravy. If you dislike these flavors, omit the nutmeg and use a regular pork breakfast sausage instead of the sage-flavored variety.

One of the differences you'll find when you talk to people about how they make sausage gravy is whether they make a traditional roux (just drippings and flour), or whether they add the flour directly to the sausage after it's browned. I've made it both ways; the gravy thickens up just fine when you add the flour to the browned sausage mixture.

SAUSAGE GRAVY

Ingredients
1 lb. sage-flavored pork sausage
¼ cup finely chopped white or yellow onion
6 tablespoon all purpose flour
4 cups whole milk
½ teaspoon poultry seasoning
½ teaspoon ground nutmeg
¼ teaspoon salt
1-2 dashes of Worcestershire sauce
1-2 dashes of Tabasco sauce, cayenne pepper, or
    other hot sauce
1-2 tablespoon butter or bacon grease (if needed)

Instructions

Preheat a 4-quart saucepan over medium-high heat (put a few drops of water in the pan—when they evaporate, you know the pan is ready). Crumble the sausage into the pan and let it brown for a minute or two, then turn down to medium heat. Continue cooking, breaking up the sausage into smaller pieces, until no pink remains. Stir in the onions and cook until they are transparent.

Remove sausage with a slotted spatula or spoon, leaving the drippings in the pan. If less than 3 tablespoons of drippings remain, add enough butter (or bacon grease) to equal that amount. Add the cooked sausage back to the pan on medium heat, and sprinkle the flour over the sausage. Stir in the flour and cook for about 6-8 minutes, until the mixture starts bubbling and turns slightly golden brown.

Stir in poultry seasoning, nutmeg, Worcestershire sauce, Tabasco sauce and salt; cook for 1 minute to deepen the flavors. Slowly add the milk and cook over medium heat, stirring occasionally, until thickened (about 15 minutes). Be patient, it will thicken!

As for the biscuits, there are countless recipes that have been handed down over the years in Southern families. Many swear that White Lily Self-Rising Flour is essential to making light fluffy biscuits. However, in my experience you can make perfectly respectable biscuits even if you can't get your hands on that Southern staple. You can also mix up the ratio of butter and shortening, or just use one or the other, or lard, if you prefer.

I recommend preparing the biscuits for baking, getting the gravy started, and *then* baking them, while the gravy is thickening up. That way you can stir the gravy frequently, which is hard to do when your hands are covered with flour and dough. If you don't have self-rising flour, you can substitute using a ratio of 1 cup all-purpose flour, 1 1/4 teaspoon baking powder, plus 1/8 teaspoon of salt, for every cup of self-rising flour.

BUTTERMILK BISCUITS

Ingredients

2 ½ cups self-rising flour (plus extra for flouring
  your work surface)
2 teaspoons sugar (optional)
½ tsp kosher salt
4 tablespoons vegetable shortening (see baking tips, below)
4 tablespoons butter (chilled)
1 cup chilled buttermilk (plus 1-2 tablespoons more, if
  needed)
1 tablespoon melted butter (optional, to brush on top of
  biscuits after baking)

Instructions

Preheat oven to 450 degrees F. Prepare a floured surface for shaping the dough and have an ungreased baking sheet ready (lined with Silpat sheets if you have them).

Whisk together flour, sugar and salt in a medium-sized bowl. Using a fork or a pastry blender, cut in the shortening and butter. Work quickly, you don't want the fats to melt—the key to fluffy biscuits is minimal handling. The mixture should be crumbly.

Make a well in the flour mixture, and pour in the buttermilk. Stir with a spoon and blend just until the liquid is absorbed and the dough comes away from the sides of the bowl; add 1-2 tablespoons more buttermilk if the dough is dry. Do not over mix; the dough will be tacky, neither wet nor dry.

With lightly floured hands, turn out the dough onto a lightly floured surface and gently fold it over on itself 2 or 3 times. Shape into a 3/4" thick round. If you use a rolling pin, be sure to flour it first, to keep the dough from sticking to the pin.

Using a 2-inch biscuit cutter, cut out the biscuits, pressing straight down (avoid the temptation to twist the cutter, as twisting keeps the biscuits from rising). Dip the cutter in flour between cuttings to keep the dough from sticking to the cutter. Place biscuits on the baking sheet so that they just touch (for crunchy sides, leave space in between). Reshape the leftover dough and continue cutting. Remember to handle the dough as little as possible.

Bake for 15-18 minutes, or until the biscuits are lightly golden brown on top. Turn the baking sheet around halfway through baking.

*Optional: brush the tops of the biscuits with melted butter.

*Baking Tips:
1) Spoon the flour into your measuring cup, and level it off with the back side of a knife. If you scoop the flour, it will pack into the measuring cup, yielding too much flour.
2) Instead of 4 tablespoons each of butter and shortening, feel free to use 8 tablespoons of shortening or butter, or any combination up to 8 tablespoons.

BAKED GARLIC CHEESE GRITS

Ingredients
6 cups chicken broth
1 teaspoon salt
¼ teaspoon pepper
¼ teaspoon garlic powder
2 cups regular grits
16 ounces Cheddar, cubed
½ cup milk
4 large eggs, beaten
½ cup (1 stick) unsalted butter
8 ounces grated sharp white Cheddar

Instructions
Preheat the oven to 350 degrees F. Grease a 4-quart casserole dish.

Bring the broth, salt, pepper, and garlic powder to a boil in a 2-quart saucepan. Stir in the grits, and whisk until completely combined. Reduce the heat to low and simmer until the grits are thick, about 8 to 10 minutes.

Add the cubed Cheddar and milk and stir. Gradually stir in the eggs and butter, stirring until all are combined. Pour the mixture into the prepared casserole dish. Sprinkle with the white Cheddar and bake for 35 to 40 minutes or until set.

Chapter 18

REVOLVING DOOR

Although I had found myself starting to enjoy the continual interaction with my guests—a definite change for the recluse in me—the warm weather brought with it more guests and many new challenges, making me wonder again whether I'd made the right decision to open an inn.

It was June four months later, and all five of my guestrooms were booked for three weeks straight. Sounds good, doesn't it? And it was. I was happy to have all the business, especially after having absolutely no bookings in December and just a trickle in January.

I should have been overjoyed when we booked almost sixty rooms in February. But most of those bookings were for two in a room, sometimes three, so that meant approximately 150-175 people revolving in and out of my front door. That's 150 breakfasts to make, maybe 150 loads of sheets, towels, and pillowcases to wash, and endless dirty toilets to clean, beds to make, and so on. I honestly didn't mind doing the housework and I loved to cook, especially breakfast. But sometimes it got to be a little much, and at times my life was a blur.

Aleksander House wasn't just a bed and breakfast, it was my home. But sometimes I felt like it had been taken over by another planet—a planet of incessant travelers hell-bent on making my life complicated.

Now mind you, there was a definite upside to having all these guests—namely, that I'd be able to cover my expenses and maybe have a little left over to go out to dinner with a girlfriend. Also, having guests from all over the world was interesting, fun, and stimulating. We'd had people from Germany, England, Ireland, Australia, and China, as well as many others from all over the US. I loved that, and most everybody had been gracious and friendly. But by June of that year, I was exhausted.

My work schedule was around twelve hours a day, seven days a week. By that time, I'd started writing seriously again, so this included my writing time, to which I devoted approximately four hours a day. I usually got out of bed in the morning between 5:30 and 6:30 A.M., and the first thing I did was run downstairs and make coffee and tea for my guests. After that I'd sneak a cup of coffee for myself and run back upstairs to check my e-mail. At 7:00 A.M., I would go back down to the kitchen and start breakfast. Hopefully, that was when my housekeeper showed up.

You never knew who was going to come through the revolving door until they were there, standing before you in your parlor. Another reason why being a risk-taker and an almost fearless person is an advantage in this business.

Around the middle of June, a lady called and booked one of my two-room suites for herself and her four sisters. They were to check in on July 8 and stay for five nights. Nice booking, eh? Yes, it was—and I held it for them for a whole two weeks. This was our busy season, and calls were coming in right and left to book that suite for the exact dates Mrs. Hampton wanted. I can't remember how many people I turned away.

On July 8, at precisely 3 P.M., the door bell began to ring, over and over. I started down the forty stairs to the first floor. By the time I got to the door, the bell had stopped ringing. I opened it just in time to see two middle-aged ladies walking back to their car.

"Hi," I called, and waved to them. They looked at each other and both came marching back up to the front door.

"We're not staying!" one of them announced.

"Why not?" I asked.

"Because this place is a ghetto," she snapped.

My jaw dropped maybe fifty feet, and for a few seconds I was speechless. Of course she had put me on the defensive, but before I could launch into my best spiel about what a great inn I had and how Old Louisville was an historic neighborhood—the third-largest preservation area in the country, with more Victorian houses and stained glass than any other city—she came out with: "People were honking horns at us, and we saw a Negro."

With that remark, I started getting angry. Then Mrs. Hampton took her hand, wiped it down the outside of my house, and rubbed the dirt together between her forefinger and thumb. She held two dirty fingers up and looked at me with a smirk, as if to say, "See how dirty your house is?"

Still on the defensive, I said, "It's the outside of the house, of course it's dirty. And it's been raining a lot—"

I don't know why I added the thing about the rain. Anyhow, I didn't have a chance to finish what I was saying, because at that point she leaned toward me and shouted, "I want my credit card back!"

Backing up, I replied, "I don't have your credit card."

"Yes you do. I gave it to you over the phone," she said.

"You gave me the number, yes, and I am going to charge you 50 percent for not cancelling within the time limit spelled out in my cancellation policy," I said. "It was written in the confirmation letter I sent you."

Well, they both nearly fainted at that.

After arguing for another three or four minutes, the two of them turned and scurried down the walk to their car, all the time threatening me with calls to the Better Business Bureau, the Louisville B&B association, and the Kentucky B&B association. I went up to my room to recover from the shock of just having lost over $1,000 in revenue.

I just may have to pay back the 50 percent I charged to the card for a deposit, I thought. I knew they would probably dispute the charge, and the outcome would depend upon whether or not the credit card company considered their dispute legitimate. I, of course, would have an opportunity to defend my actions.

Fortunately, I ended up rebooking all but one of the nights Mrs. Hampton had reserved, so I was able to refund her for four days without taking a financial hit. I kept the deposit for the one day I didn't book, however.

A few days later, a couple of guys checked in with their dog and stayed three days. While they were there, they let the dog poop all over the backyard and didn't pick it up—which I discovered one week later, after stepping in it.

In early September, three people from China checked in to stay for two weeks in one room with a roll-away. There was the father, a school headmaster in his forties, the mother, who looked around sixteen, and a four-year-old son. They slept all day, wouldn't let us clean the room, ate pizza in their room every night, and came down to breakfast a half-hour to an hour late each morning, demanding foods we didn't have.

When I asked them if my housekeeper could get in to clean their room at some point, the father/school headmaster/pain-in the-neck replied that he wasn't about to work around the house-keeper's schedule. So we asked him for his schedule, saying we'd work around that. He said okay, but never gave it to us. Meanwhile, they let their four-year-old stay up till midnight every night, yelling and screaming and jumping up and down on the bed. To say the least, they were unusually hostile and inconsiderate guests.

Later in the week, while the family from China was still there, two couples checked into the suite on the third floor. They had a thirteen-year-old dog and a cat with them. The first day they were there, they left the poor dog in the room for twelve hours while they went out gambling. He, as you might expect, peed all over the rugs. As for the cat, they put its litter box up on the cane trunk at the foot of the bed, which meant that every time the cat got into the box, the litter fell down through the spaces in the woven cane and settled on the sheets and towels inside.

Of course we took care of everything, including rolling up the peed-on carpet and taking it to the cleaners and moving the cat's litter box to the hearth of the fireplace. That's what innkeepers do. And with smiles on our faces, no less. We had also managed at this point to sneak into the headmaster's room and clean it while he and his family were eating breakfast, which made me feel a little better.

Eventually, I started charging for cleaning and breakage, and added on a pet fee.

The day the Chinese family left, an opera director and his wife checked in. He had fallen down the stairs before he arrived and so spent the three days he was there in bed. We brought him a heating pad, cold packs, hot tea, and aspirin every day, trying to keep him comfortable.

This is a sample of the way things sometimes went at the inn. It's hard to plan on anything, and you never know what's going to happen next. Have I said yet that an innkeeper needs to be extremely flexible?

Mrs. Hampton wasn't the only guest who ever arrived at my inn and decided they didn't want to stay. One beautiful fall day I was in the garden when I heard the faint ring of the front doorbell. By the time I got there someone was banging on the door.

When I opened the door, a young couple with very stern

looks on their faces stood glaring at me. The woman also looked a little frightened.

"We have reservations, but my wife doesn't want to stay here," the young man said timidly.

"Come on in for a minute," I said.

I thought if I showed them around my beautiful inn and assured them there was no problem and told them the neighborhood was safe, they would be just fine.

The woman's eyes darted quickly around the room. "We live in the country," she said. "And I'm not used to the city. I don't want to stay here."

When I told her I would have to charge them for the night, her whole demeanor changed. She no longer appeared shy and reticent. In fact, her face took on a bright red hue and her body went into action. I told her that I'd sent her a confirmation letter stating that you must cancel at least seventy-two hours prior to arrival time—which they hadn't—to avoid charges of one night's stay or 50 percent of the total cost.

"You mean you're actually going to charge us one hundred and twenty dollars?"

"Yes, ma'am. That's our policy," I said.

At that, the woman went into anger/attack mode. She got right up in my face and began yelling at the top of her lungs.

"That's outrageous," she said "I'm not leaving here until you tell me you're not going to charge us for tonight," she screamed.

"Sorry, but I've already put the charges through," I said, as calmly as possible.

At that, she went absolutely ballistic and started calling me all kinds of names, screaming, "You stupid bitch, @#$%&, gimme my money back! Gimme my money back! Now! I'm not leaving until you do!"

She backed off for a moment, then lunged at me. I thought she was going to hit me. She was obviously trying to intimidate me, but I didn't back down.

"You'll have to leave now," I said, trying to appear calm though my nerves were rattled. I still didn't back down, although I was thinking about it by now. I asked them again to leave, but she refused. In fact, she announced that she was going to call the police on me. All this time, her husband never said a word.

When the police knocked on the door, I ushered them in and stood back to see how they were going to handle the situation. The woman rushed up to one of the policemen and started rattling off her story, making me out to be a crook and a shrew. I tried to get a word or two in to defend myself, but soon the room was teeming with accusations.

Finally the police separated us and listened to both of our stories. They told her they couldn't force me to give her money back, and they couldn't arrest me like she wanted them to. Then they informed her she would have to leave the premises. I breathed a sigh of relief as the door slammed shut, hoping I'd never see her again.

The amount of fear this young couple exhibited really caught me off guard. And I found it puzzling. But when I reflected on it, I realized they were not the first of my guests who had appeared to be frightened by the city. Most of them lived in the country or at least the suburbs. But it constantly amazed me, probably because I have always lived right in the city. I love the city. And I honestly don't think the city is any more dangerous than the suburbs. I know there are plenty of people who will disagree with me, and that's okay, but I know I couldn't live my life that way—in constant fear every time I left home. Seems like a waste of time. Our cities have so much to offer, and life is too short not to take advantage of it. I refuse to give into the paranoia. I know you can never be sure, but I think I'd rather trust that everything will be all right than isolate myself, making myself lonely and disconnected, out of fear.

Although that year brought some interesting challenges, I was getting better at handling a variety of sticky situations, and wasn't so dependent on Bryan anymore. I had been in business nearly twelve years and I had learned to deal with the unexpected in an efficient manner and not let it throw me off my game—the goal of every respectable innkeeper.

And to remind me of those past sticky situations, I've included my guests' favorite below. Although work-intensive, they are absolutely amazing. And they freeze well.

Recipe

Sticky Buns
(makes 9)

DOUGH

Ingredients
⅔ cup whole milk
5 tablespoons sugar, divided
1¾ teaspoons active dry yeast (from one ¼-ounce envelope)
2 large eggs, room temperature
2¾ cups all-purpose flour
1 teaspoon salt
½ cup (1 stick) unsalted butter, cut into 1-inch pieces,
    room temperature, plus ½ tablespoon, melted

Instructions
Heat milk in a small saucepan over medium heat, or in a micro-wave, until an instant-read thermometer registers 110°–115°.

Transfer milk to a 2-cup measuring cup; stir in 1 tablespoon sugar. Sprinkle yeast over milk and whisk to blend. Let sit until yeast is foamy, about 5 minutes. Add eggs; whisk until smooth.

Combine flour, salt, and remaining 4 tablespoons. sugar in the bowl of a stand mixer fitted with a dough hook. Add milk mixture.

With mixer running, add ½ cup room-temperature butter, 1 piece at a time, blending well between additions. Mix on medium speed 1 minute. Knead on medium-high speed until dough is soft and silky, about 5 minutes.

Brush a medium bowl with about 1 teaspoon melted butter; place dough in bowl. Brush top of dough with remaining melted butter; cover with plastic wrap. Let rise in a warm, draft-free area until doubled in size, 1–1½ hours. Chill dough 2 hours.

TOPPING

Ingredients
1¾ cups chopped pecans (about 8 ounces)
½ cup (1 stick) unsalted butter
¾ cup (packed) dark brown sugar
¾ cup heavy cream
⅓ cup honey
¼ teaspoon salt

Instructions
Preheat oven to 350°. Spread nuts on a rimmed baking sheet. Toast until fragrant and slightly darkened, 10–12 minutes. Let cool completely. Set 1¼ cups nuts aside for buns.

Melt butter in a small heavy saucepan over medium heat. Stir in brown sugar, cream, honey, and salt. Bring to a boil, reduce heat to medium, and simmer until glaze is golden brown and glossy, 3–4 minutes.

Pour 1 cup glaze into baking pan, tilting to coat bottom and sides. Set aside remaining glaze. Sprinkle ½ cup toasted pecans over bottom of baking pan and let cool.

BUNS

Ingredients
½ cup (1 stick) unsalted butter, room temperature
½ cup (packed) dark brown sugar
¾ teaspoon ground cinnamon
½ teaspoon grated nutmeg
⅛ teaspoon salt
All-purpose flour (for dusting)
1 large egg
Coarse sea salt

Instructions

With an electric mixer on medium speed, beat butter, sugar, cinnamon, nutmeg, and salt in a medium bowl until light and fluffy (2-3 minutes). Set filling aside.

Roll out dough on a lightly floured work surface; work into a 12x16" rectangle about ¼" thick. Arrange dough on work surface so long side faces you. Spread cinnamon-sugar mixture over dough, leaving a 1" border on the side farthest from you.

Sprinkle ¾ cup chopped pecans over cinnamon-sugar mixture. Beginning with the long edge closest to you, roll dough into a log, tightening as you go and patting in the ends. Pinch together the seam where the long side meets the roll to seal. Arrange log seam side down.

Using a large knife, cut log crosswise into 9 pieces (lightly flour knife between slices if dough is too sticky). Turn buns cut side up and gently pat top to flatten slightly. If needed, reshape to form round edges by cupping lightly floured hands around each bun and gently pushing and turning them in a circular motion. Transfer buns to prepared pan and lightly sprinkle sea salt over each, spacing them apart evenly (buns should not touch each other).

Loosely cover pan with plastic wrap or a kitchen towel. Let buns rise in a warm, draft-free area until doubled in size, 45 minutes to an hour, or 1½ to 2 hours if dough has been chilled overnight.

Arrange a rack in middle of oven; preheat to 350°. Whisk egg with ½ teaspoon water in a small bowl. Brush tops of buns with egg wash.

Bake, rotating pan halfway through, and tenting with foil if browning too quickly, until buns are golden brown, filling is bubbling, and an instant-read thermometer inserted into center of buns registers 185°, about 50 minutes. Let cool 5 minutes. Spoon remaining glaze over top and sprinkle with ½ cup pecans. Let cool in pan on a wire rack.Serve buns warm or at room temperature.

Chapter 19

KELLY AND THE TRUCK SHOW

We continued to be busy through the fall. Christmas came and went before I knew it; the years seemed to be going by increasingly quickly. The Mid-America Trucking Show was just around the corner again.

One morning, the secretary of one of the large trucking companies in Chicago called to reserve a room for herself. I booked her into the last available room, which meant I would be sleeping in the back hall on the first floor again for a few days. She gave me a credit card number that she later said belonged to her grandmother—a little unusual, but I checked it out and it was approved. That did it: I was fully booked! The show was less than a week away, but that gave me plenty of time to shop for the extra food I needed to feed nine truckers and a secretary.

People started checking in around four P.M. the day before the show started. I had a couple of repeats from the year before, and four new guys from New Jersey who pulled out cigars the second they got inside the door. "Sorry, fellas, you can't smoke those stogies in here," I said lightly. "My inn is smoke free—but I have a deck out back!"

The weather was still a little chilly, but I figured the March winds wouldn't deter these guys from further blackening their lungs with their ever-lovin' Havanas. There was extra beer in the dining room fridge again, and I was sure they'd make good use of that too.

By seven P.M., everyone had checked in except Kelly, the secretary. I had booked her into Roxanne's Room, a beautiful, sunny yellow room with white Battenberg lace curtains and dust ruffles, overlooking the garden. She finally arrived at ten P.M., just before my bedtime.

When I answered the door, I found her peering into her shoulder bag, as she rifled around for something deep inside. The drizzling rain had dampened her rain coat and her short curly blond hair glistened under the porch light. She glanced up for a minute.

"I'm looking for my reservation," she said, wiping away a raindrop which had made its way down the left side of her nose onto her cheek. She continued searching through her purse. "I'm Kelly," she said. A gust of wind brushed against her legs, causing her to shiver slightly.

"Can I come in?" she asked.

"Oh sure, sorry. Let me help you."

She gathered up her belongings and, giving it a kick with one foot, pulled her overstuffed suitcase over the threshold. I watched her as she stood shaking her head. A mist of tiny rain-drops fell to the carpet beneath her feet while she wiped her face dry with the scarf around her shoulders. She was small, pale, and quite attractive. I couldn't help fixating on her bright blue eyes. I watched her as she reached into her purse again and pulled out a folded paper the size of an envelope.

"Sorry to get here so late. My flight was delayed. Here's my reservation slip and my grandmother's credit card. Just don't run it through, I'll pay in cash when I check out." She said, extending her hand to me.

"Okay. Let me just get your room key; will you be having breakfast in the morning?"

"Yes, definitely. What time do you serve it?"

"We do an eight o'clock and a nine o'clock."

"Great! I'll do the nine o'clock."

After showing Kelly to her room, I went into the kitchen to fix myself a cup of chamomile tea. Around ten minutes later I heard the front door slam shut. I hurried to the parlor window just in time to see her get into a sleek black Mercedes that sped off with her inside. She had changed her clothes, discarded the running shoes she'd had on, and changing into very high heels. *Pretty late for a planning meeting*, I thought, but was too tired to think any more about it.

Exhausted after a long day, I fell asleep on my cot in the hallway and didn't wake till the alarm went off at six A.M. Bryan had come in the back door and was already in the kitchen when I woke.

After breakfast, we went up to clean the rooms. Kelly's towels were on the floor in the bathroom, her white washcloths completely covered with makeup, lipstick, and lots of black mascara. I knew it wouldn't all come out in the wash. *There goes another set of expensive towels,* I thought. I set a jar of cotton balls and makeup remover on the sink, hoping she'd get the hint. The door to the closet was open, and I couldn't help but notice the sexy little numbers inside. *Why would a secretary be dressed like that at a trade show?* I wondered.

When we went up to clean rooms the next morning, the washcloths in Kelly's room were again covered in makeup. There were also whiskey bottles under the bed, and male underwear between the sheets. This time, I left her a note telling her not to use the washcloths for makeup, and not to bring her boyfriend and alcohol up to her room. I would have just told her to leave, but she hadn't paid the bill yet. I knew she wouldn't be home till late, so I figured I'd talk to her in the morning.

Morning came and Kelly did not come down to breakfast. I went up to her room and opened the door to discover she was gone, two days early—skipped out in the middle of the night. The room had been emptied of all her belongings. I was concerned about the bill. She had given me her grandmother's credit card, but told me not to run it through—that she would pay me in cash when she checked out. Of course, she hadn't.

I talked to the truckers after Kelly left and found out that she was an exotic dancer, there to entertain them. I have no idea how many of them she entertained in my guestroom, but now I certainly understood how she was planning to come up with the cash to pay the bill.

Fortunately, Grandma's credit card went through. With the Farm Machinery Show and the Trucking Show over again for another year, I looked forward to the warmer weather.

Recipe

Grandma's Oatmeal Cookies
(makes 4 dozen)

Ingredients
1 cup (2 sticks) margarine or butter, softened
1 cup granulated sugar
1 cup firmly packed brown sugar
2 eggs
1 teaspoon vanilla
2 cups all-purpose flour
1 teaspoon baking soda
1 teaspoon ground cinnamon
½ teaspoon salt (optional)
¼ teaspoon ground nutmeg
3 cups oats (uncooked)
1 cup raisins

Instructions
Pre-heat oven to 375°F.

In a large bowl, cream margarine or butter and sugars until creamy.

Add egg and vanilla and beat well.

Add combined flour, baking soda, cinnamon, salt and nutmeg. Mix well.

Add oats and mix well.

Drop dough by rounded tablespoonfuls onto greased cookie sheets.

Bake 10 to 12 minutes, for a crisp cookie.

Cool on cookie sheets, and then move to wire racks and cool completely.

Chapter 20

WILL THE REAL
ROGER EASTON STAND UP?

I was on the third floor of my house, sitting at my computer with my shoes off, working on a new article. By the time I finished the last paragraph, what had started as an ordinary knock at the door had turned into a steady pounding. I got up and walked to the stairway, shoes in hand. Sitting on the top stair, I put them on one at a time as the pounding getting louder and louder and took on a sense of urgency. I hurried down the forty stairs to the ground floor, thinking that this must be the worker from the street who had come by earlier to tell me they were turning my water off for a while.

I opened the front door and there stood a rumpled-looking man, his weather-beaten canvas jacket open in the front, revealing a denim work shirt. His hair was all askew, and a backpack was thrown over his left shoulder. He looked a little annoyed.

"Sorry," I said, "It's a big house . . . over four thousand square feet. It takes a while to get to the door. Can I help you?"

"Yeah," he said, "I'm here to check in."

Checkin? Checkin? I thought, my mind racing. *Did I have a check-in today? Oh my God, I think I did! But I didn't think it would be this dirty construction worker.* I finally gathered my wits and said, "And you are . . . Mister . . .?"

"Evans," he said brusquely, "the businessman from Virginia."

Businessman? That's a laugh. This guy is no businessman, I thought. *Where is his briefcase and computer?*

I kept my skepticism off my face. "Mr. Evans, of course." I smiled. "Do come in."

"And you are?" he asked as he stepped through the door, reeking of tobacco.

"I'm Nancy, the owner and innkeeper here. Go ahead and put your backpack down here," I said, gesturing to the hall, "and I'll show you around."

I took him into the parlor to give him the grand tour, the one I always did for my incoming overnight guests. As we left the parlor and entered the dining room, I noticed him giving the entire room a once-over.

"Is it okay if I have some of that liquor over in the corner?" he asked, completely ignoring the plate of freshly baked chocolate chip cookies on the table.

After hesitating for a bit to think that one over, I answered, "Yes."

I'm such a trusting soul.

He told me he would be eating breakfast at nine and asked if his friend, the one who had made the reservation—Roger—could stop by later for a visit.

As we completed the tour, he asked, "Is there anyone else here but me?"

I thought seriously about lying, but answered honestly: "No."

"Do you live here alone?" he asked.

A sharp jab in my stomach alerted me. *Do I tell him the truth? Why is he asking that?*

"Yes," I said and sent him up to the third floor with a key to find his room.

I hurried to my room on the second floor and double-locked the door. Sitting on the bed, I tried to catch my breath, his words whirling around in my head. Later I heard him leave, then return. I quietly went down to the first floor to check out what was going on. I entered the parlor and there he was with an already half-empty bottle of vodka in his hand, pouring himself a drink. The brown paper sack from the liquor store across the street was lying on the floor.

"Hi," he said, looking up at me from my favorite wingback chair. He had a crooked but friendly smile on his face. He now reeked of both tobacco *and* vodka.

"Hi," I said, scurrying past him and heading for the kitchen.

"Like a drink?"

"Oh no, thank you. I don't drink," I said—maybe a little too curtly, but I wasn't interested in continuing the conversation.

I made it to the kitchen, happy that I wouldn't have to answer any more personal questions, and relatively confident that I'd escaped without appearing too rude. I retreated up the back stairs to my room, which I immediately locked tight. An hour or so later, the doorbell rang and I heard Mr. Evans open it and greet his friend. For a while, it was very quiet, and then I heard the two of them leave.

I finished watching the evening news and went downstairs to make myself some dinner. I walked into the parlor and was a little taken aback by the empty vodka bottle plopped down on the antique table next to the chair where Mr. Evans had been sitting. After I recovered and threw out the empty vodka bottle, I had dinner and retired to my room for the rest of the evening. I talked myself into believing everything would be okay and I wasn't in any imminent danger. Then I double-locked the door again, grabbed the phone, and went to bed.

The next morning I was up bright and early, making freshly ground coffee, when I heard Mr. Evans coming down the stairs. As he walked into the dining room, I was surprised to see how good he looked in the morning light.

"Thought you'd have a little trouble getting up for breakfast this morning," I said.

"Why's that?" he asked.

I didn't want to be rude, but decided to tell him what I thought. "Well, you had quite a bit to drink last night. You finished that whole bottle of vodka."

"Oh that was nothing," he said, laughing. "I'm a pretty seasoned drinker."

Seasoned drinker? I thought. *More like an alcoholic, if you ask me.* I half-expected him to ask for a Bloody Mary for breakfast.

"I'm starving," he said.

"Well go ahead and grab yourself a cup of coffee or tea," I said, "and I'll have your breakfast ready for you soon!"

Back in the kitchen, I cooked up my fabulous scrambled eggs, sourdough toast, and bacon and loaded it all up on a tray. Then I took a deep breath and headed back into the dining room.

"It looks great," Mr. Evans said appreciatively when I walked in with the food. "Will you join me?" He gestured to the seat across from him.

I took the seat he indicated, wondering just how this man could have the gall to ask if I lived here alone. We exchanged some pleasantries, and then he asked another of his unexpected questions.

"You know," he began, "the jails are jam-packed with prisoners."

"Uh-huh." I nodded and gobbled up some of my wonderful eggs.

"How do you feel about that?" he asked.

"About what?" I was confused.

"About all those prisoners?" he said.

Oh my God, I thought, *he's not trying to get me into a conversation where I expose my position and then he jumps on me and shoves his obsessive ideas down my throat, is he? How do I get out of this?*

"Well . . . I . . . I don't usually get into these kinds of conversations," I stuttered, "especially at breakfast."

I managed to change the subject. But he just kept on trying to hook me into similar conversations—politics, religion, anything controversial he could think of. Finally, when he realized I wasn't going to be drawn in, he gave up and began talking about himself. He told me that he was an inventor, and as our conversation continued, I could tell that he was quite creative and intelligent. He told me he had invented a very hard plastic, which had made him the millionaire he was today. Then the conversation turned to Roger, his friend . . . the one who'd helped him finish off an entire bottle of vodka before dinner last night.

"Roger's a good friend of mine," he said. "He's actually an inventor as well."

"Oh, yes?" I said. "Has he invented anything notable?"

"Yes," he said, "Roger is the one who invented the GPS."

After nearly choking on my eggs, I repeated, "The GPS?" *Was this guy for real?* "The GPS that you put in your car to tell you how to get from one place to another?"

"That's the one," he said nonchalantly.

"How come I've never heard of him?" I asked. "What's his last name?" In my head, I was already online, googling "GPS."

"His name is Roger Easton," he answered.

I was suddenly jerked back to reality by the sound of the front doorbell. I quickly ran to the door and flung it open. And there he was. Roger. Creator of the GPS. Master inventor. Savior of the navigationally impaired. In all his glory.

"Roger, is it?" I asked.

He nodded.

"I'm Nancy. Come on in. Want a cup of coffee?"

I never asked Roger directly about his invention; I didn't want to embarrass him, in case it wasn't true. And Mr. Evans said no more on the subject. But this is what I found on Google:

"The evidence shows that Roger Easton invented the GPS and is finally getting credit for it, as shown by his receiving the National Medal of Technology (below). Brad Parkinson deserves much credit

for his successful development of the system, but neither Brad Par-
kinson nor Ivan Getting (who also had been given credit) invented
it. Further study about GPS has reinforced prior understanding
that the Navy had the technology and the Air Force had the money
to fund it."

I quickly scanned the page to see if the Roger Easton I'd had coffee with that morning at the breakfast table was the man pictured. It was not. It was a different Roger Easton. The one who had actually invented the GPS.

I don't know who Mr. Evans really introduced to me to that morning, and I guess I never will.

A well-made omelet is a magnificent thing. It's soft and custard-like, golden-yellow, and best eaten while still piping hot from the skillet. An omelet makes a fantastic breakfast seasoned with just salt and pepper, but it also can be eaten for lunch or dinner with anything from diced ham, veggies, and cheese to sautéed mushrooms.

There are two tricks to making a great omelet. First, **use a nonstick skillet**. This is one of the few times when we truly recommend a pan like this—it just makes the whole process of quickly cooking the eggs and sliding them onto the plate a million times easier. A small, well-seasoned cast-iron skillet will also do the job. If you don't have either of these pieces of cookware, then use a little extra butter in your pan.

The second trick is to **cook the omelet until it looks just *under* done**. The bottom should be firm and set, but the top should still look a little wet. If you wait until the top is dry, then your omelet will be dry — and that is no one's idea of a good breakfast. But if you're not a fan of runny eggs, don't worry; the eggs will finish cooking in the residual heat after you fold it.

From start to finish, an omelet should take you no more than a minute or two. It really is a quick-cooking dish (another reason omelets are a great breakfast or quick midweek dinner)! If you're adding fillings to your omelet, just make sure those are cooked or re-warmed, if needed, and ready to go before you actually start making the omelet. When that omelet is done, you want to be able to add the fillings, fold the omelet over, and eat it right away.

Making a great omelet takes practice, so don't worry if your first few attempts end up looking more like scrambled eggs. No harm done—they're just eggs!—and you'll get better each time you try.

Recipe

A Perfect French Omelet

Ingredients
3 large eggs
Salt and pepper to taste
1 tablespoon butter

Instructions
In a medium bowl, beat eggs with a disposable plastic or reusable wooden fork just until the last traces of white are mixed in; season with salt and pepper.

In an unscratched 8-inch nonstick skillet, melt butter, swirling over moderate heat, until fully melted and foamy but not browned. Add eggs and stir rapidly with fork, tines up, while shaking pan to agitate eggs; make sure to move fork all around pan to break up curds and scrape them from bottom of skillet as they form. Stop stirring as soon as eggs are very softly scrambled and creamy (but still loose enough to come together into a single mass), 1 to 2 minutes.

Using fork, gently spread egg in an even layer around skillet and scrape down any wispy bits around the edges. The top surface should be loose and creamy, but if it looks too liquid and raw, cook undisturbed for another few seconds. (If it still flows, you can swirl skillet to send loose egg to the edges, where it will set more quickly.)

Remove from heat, tilt skillet up by its handle, and, using fork, gently roll omelette down over itself until it is nearly folded in half. Using fork, push omelette to edge of skillet so that lower edge of egg begins to just barely overhang; use fork to fold up the overhanging edge, closing the omelet.

Hold skillet over plate and turn omelet out onto it. It should be almond- or cigar-shaped, with the seam on bottom; if it's not, lay a clean kitchen towel over it and use your hands to adjust its shape and position, then remove towel. Serve. (To make another omelet, wipe any eggy bits out of skillet and repeat.)

Chapter 21

DOWN THE BACK STAIRS

I stepped out into the air and dropped like a heavy bolt of silk cloth . . . down, down, down. Alice's rabbit hole flashing before me. When I landed, the pain took over. It was excruciating. Lying there in the dim light, barely able to breathe, I managed to roll over on my stomach. Tears slithered onto the tile floor. I lay there for what seemed like a very long time.

I had landed on my left side, my foot turned under me, cookies and glass of cold milk thrown across the hallway. I had been on my way to my bedroom, up the steep back stairway, when the fire alarm suddenly went off. I had quickly turned, trying to get back down as fast as I could to turn off the alarm before the fire department came rushing into my house.

I thought I was on the first step. Unfortunately, I was on the fifth.

The piercing sound of the alarm cut through the silence and darkness of the first floor. I was lying on the hall floor outside the kitchen, the only light a dim yellow ribbon coming from the front hallway. I rolled over on my back and tried to gather my senses.

I tried to get up, but my whole body told me not to move. I knew that if I didn't get to the alarm soon, the fire department would start hacking down the front door.

"Hello! . . . system alert . . . battery okay; Hello! . . . system alert . . . battery okay." The wall monitor kept spitting out the status of the system.

Rolling back to my stomach, I pushed myself up onto my knees so I could crawl to the alarm box. The pain in my left foot was bad, and my eyes were blurred from gushing tears. I got to the wall and pulled myself up to where the security box was attached. I tried to turn off the alarm, but in my state of shock I couldn't remember the code number. I knew it was my dog's birthday, so I kept trying it over and over, punching in combinations of various numbers. All of a sudden, the alarm stopped. I don't know how I did it, but I finally got the numbers right.

I slid back down the wall and crawled to the phone. A searing pain ripped up my left side as I dialed, but I managed to get my friend Valerie on the line.

She didn't hesitate a moment when I told her what had happened. "We'll be right there," she said, and hung up.

Not being able to put any weight on my foot, I crawled to the front door and reached up and unlocked it. Then I plopped myself on the bottom step of the long staircase and waited.

Within fifteen minutes, Valerie and her husband, Craig, pushed their way through the doorway. By that time, my left foot was so swollen I could barely remove my shoe and sock. It was turning dark purple and black, and blue streaks were climbing up my calf. My ankle had disappeared into the bloated mass that used to be my foot.

They called the paramedics, who lifted me onto a stretcher and carried me out to the ambulance. By that time, I had severe muscle cramps in my leg all the way up to my thigh and was in a lot of pain. The paramedics checked my vitals but said they couldn't give me anything to take the edge off. I'd have to wait till we got to the hospital.

While I was lying on a hospital cart in the emergency room, Valerie and Craig by my side, a woman wearing a blue two-piece cotton uniform and white shoes came in, walked over to the hospital cart, and laid her hand on my ankle.

"Looks pretty bad. What'd you do to yourself?" she asked.

"Well, I . . . "

She exerted some pressure on the area just above my almost totally black foot. "Does this hurt?"

I burst into tears and couldn't utter a word. *Does it hurt? You've got to be kidding.*

"Yes, it hurts. Be careful of my leg, too," I finally managed. "I have fibromyalgia. Can I have something for the pain?"

"We have to examine you first and evaluate the situation."

Evaluate the situation? My foot was deep purple, almost black and part of the bone was protruding. *What's to evaluate? I broke my damned foot. Isn't that obvious?* I couldn't help but be irritated.

"We've got to get you to x-ray as soon as possible," the nurse said.

"Why as soon as possible?"

"Because your foot is swelling rapidly, and we'll want to ice it right away."

I looked down at my throbbing foot, which by this time looked like a giant eggplant. "Valerie, I hate having you two wait for me," I said, even though I knew I couldn't get home on my own, even with a cab. *How will I get up the stairs and through the door?*

"Don't worry about it," Craig said. "Just go ahead and get it x-rayed so you know what the damage is."

A pink-coated technician wheeled a chair up and lifted me right up off the cart and into the wheelchair—thank God, 'cause I couldn't have done it myself. Putting weight on my foot was agonizing.

When we returned from x-ray, the doctor came in to give me the bad news.

"It's broken, isn't it?" I asked before he could say anything.

"Yes, you've done a fine job of breaking the metatarsal bone along the left side of your foot," he said."And spraining the ligaments all the way up to your knee, too. Does your back hurt?"

Oh my God, how am I going to run a business with a broken foot? I thought as I answered, "No, not at all. But the muscles in my leg below my knee have been in spasm this whole time."

"What about your head?"

"Nope."

"Anyplace else?"

"I'm just having a lot of muscle spasms."

"Well, we can give you a muscle relaxant for that," he said.

"And the pain in my foot?" Actually, the foot didn't hurt as much as the muscle spasms, except when I tried to put weight on it. But I wanted the medicine just in case I had trouble sleeping that night.

"We'll put a soft cast on the foot and give you some crutches," he said. "The muscle relaxants should take care of the spasms. Just give it some time. Remember to ice it every two hours. And keep it elevated as much as possible. The nurse will check you out, and if you need anything you can call your orthopedic doctor. I see you've been going to Dr. Shay. Good man. Call and make an appointment with him as soon as possible."

Craig left to pull the car up outside. The pink coat came back, helped me on with the cast, and lifted me into the wheelchair. When we got to the door of the driveway, Craig was waiting with the door open and helped me into the front seat. My foot was throbbing slightly, and the muscle spasms and pain started to increase again.

"I'll stay with you tonight," Valerie said from the backseat.

I didn't want to impose on them anymore that night. It was three A.M., and they owned a bed and breakfast too; I was pretty sure they had to make breakfast the next morning for their guests, just like I did. And I knew Alison was coming to work tomorrow, so I was okay with them leaving me alone. I probably wouldn't get much sleep either way, even with the pills they'd given me at the hospital. I was pretty distraught.

"You know what, Val?" I said. "Thanks so much for offering, but you guys have done enough for one night, and you have a business to run too. I think I'll be fine. Ali is coming in the morning."

They helped me through the door and up to the second floor. Valerie went down to the kitchen and got the ice packs I kept in the fridge. With the cast on and the crutches, at least I'd be able to get to the bathroom on my own.

The next morning, I was awake when Alison got there. When I heard her come in, I called her on her cell phone to make sure she'd come upstairs before going to the kitchen.

"Oh my gosh," she said when she saw my cast, "what happened to you?"

"Thank God you're here," I said. "I was afraid you might call in sick. I broke my foot . . . "

"How'd you ever do that?"

"It was easy. I just fell down the back stairs," I said, trying to lighten the situation with a little humor. I beckoned her over. "Sit down a minute before you start working. You know, I'm gonna need a lot of help now. Hope you're up to it, 'cause you're gonna have to run things for awhile until I recuperate. I probably won't be able to go up and down the stairs for quite a while."

"I was just thinking about that." She sounded concerned.

"Do you think you can do it on your own? Or should I get someone to come and help you?"

"I think I can do it on my own," she said. "Do we have a lot of bookings this month?"

"Hand me my green reservation book."

She went to grab it. "At least Derby is over," she said as she brought it back.

I scanned through the pages. June was always a good month,

and we did have a lot of bookings coming up. *I'd rather have Ali here than anyone else*, I thought. She'd been with me two years by that time and was one of the best assistants I'd ever had. There'd be no worries about her car breaking down or cell phone not working, and she'd always be on time.

"I'll call Erika and see if she can come in to help with the rooms," I said, "but I want you to do the baking and the breakfasts. And take care of the guests."

Ali was out of school for the summer, so it looked as though our plan would work. She set me up in the two-room suite on the second floor so I wouldn't have to go up and down the stairs, brought up the small microwave from the kitchen, and stocked both room refrigerators with food and drinks. I slept and worked in the front room and used the desk in the second room as my dining room table. I had my own little apartment, and I remained there for nearly three months, since my doctor had told me not to try to go up and down the stairs.

I managed, with the help of Alison, to see Dr. Shay a couple of times during that first month. Eventually he gave me one of those moon boot contraptions, and I set about learning to use it. I slept with it on for a week or so because it hurt so much to take it off and on. Eventually the clumsiness and warmth of it were too much for me, however, and I quit wearing it at night.

Alison was a godsend. Even so, I worried constantly about my guests and how my not being downstairs to supervise would affect my operation. I had been an innkeeper over ten years by that time, and it had been painstaking work to get to the 50-60 percent occupancy I was now used to; I didn't want to jeopardize that. I was getting a lot of repeat business and, to my own surprise, was actually turning into a pretty good businesswoman—rather ironic, considering I didn't have the right training or personality for business, and had sworn for years I'd never try it.

I had to walk with that damned moon boot on for months. It seemed like my foot took forever to heal. Dr. Shay finally prescribed physical therapy, and after finishing six weeks of it, I was as good as new—well, almost. I was able to go up and down the stairs now, albeit wearing my dreaded moon boot.

My foot did eventually heal nicely, however, and things got back to normal. Still, the experience made me start contemplating a lot of "what-ifs." I wasn't getting any younger, and although I was in very good health, the possibility of having a stroke or heart attack was always there at my age. Living alone didn't make me feel any better about that fact. I started thinking about selling the house and business and retiring again . . . maybe moving to Austin to be near Kristie.

I rarely heard from Maggie during the time my foot was healing, although I knew she spent the winters in Mexico. I did get a Christmas card from her and when she returned from Mexico in April, I made sure she remembered and was okay with my staying in her guest room again during that year's Kentucky Derby in May. I was in my seventies at the time, and the forty stairs in my house were getting a little difficult to handle, so having only one flight at Maggie's was helpful. This was actually the third time I'd come to stay with her. She never asked me to pay her anything when she first made the offer, but to reciprocate I would take her and her daughter out to dinner, or bring them Derby gifts or food from the bed and breakfast.

The night I came to stay, I was putting my things away in the guest room when I noticed there was no comforter inside the duvet cover. The weather was still cool, and I knew I would be cold without a comforter. I told her about it when we were eating the dinner I had brought from my inn, thinking she'd take care of it that evening—but later, went I went back upstairs, I saw that there still was no comforter.

Maggie came up the stairs a few minutes later to go to bed. "Hey Maggie?" I called out when I heard her on the stairs.

"Yes?" she responded, sounding faintly annoyed.

I walked out of the room. "There's still no comforter in the duvet cover," I said. "Do you think—"

"Yes, there is!"she screamed in my face.

Of course, an argument ensued. There was no comforter—I was sure of it—but Maggie wouldn't back down. She continued to scream at me, and eventually launched into a diatribe about why she didn't want me to stay overnight at her house anymore.

I was flabbergasted and, for the umpteenth time in our relationship, humiliated. Maggie was the one who asked me to come and stay there in the first place. This time, although she told me she still wanted to be friends, I ended the relationship right then and there. I was done with her abuse.

I haven't seen or heard from her since.

Since I had been stuck upstairs on the second floor for all those weeks, the thought of visiting Austin and having a fabulous meal, including dessert made by my daughter Kristi, who is a great cook, became more and more appealing. This dessert is so good and a perfect choice for the holidays.

Kristi's Lemon Cheesecake with Chocolate Cookie Crust

CRUST

Ingredients
Nonstick vegetable oil spray
6 tablespoons all-purpose flour
1 ½ teaspoons unsweetened cocoa powder
1/8 teaspoon salt
3 ounces bittersweet chocolate (54% to 60% cacao), chopped
¼ cup (½ stick) unsalted butter
¾ cup sugar
¼ cup (packed) golden brown sugar
1 large egg
½ teaspoon vanilla extract

FILLING

Ingredients
5 8-ounce packages cream cheese, room temperature
1 ¾ cups sugar
2 tablespoons all-purpose flour
1 tablespoon finely grated lemon peel
4 teaspoons fresh lemon juice
5 large eggs
2 large egg yolks
½ cup sour cream
¼ cup heavy whipping cream

TOPPING

Ingredients
1 cup sour cream
Bittersweet chocolate curls or shavings
1 lemon, halved lengthwise, thinly sliced crosswise

Instructions
Preheat oven to 350°F. Spray inside of 9-inch-diameter spring-form pan (with 2 ¾-inch-to 3-inch-high sides) with nonstick spray. Whisk flour, cocoa, and salt in small bowl; set aside.

Combine chocolate and butter in medium metal bowl; place bowl over saucepan of simmering water and stir until melted and smooth, then remove bowl. Add both sugars to chocolate mixture and whisk until blended. Let cool until mixture is barely lukewarm, about 10 minutes.

Whisk egg and vanilla into chocolate mixture. Fold flour mixture into chocolate mixture. Spread brownie batter evenly over bottom of prepared pan.

Bake brownie crust until top looks slightly cracked and a toothpick inserted into the center comes out with some moist crumbs attached, about 20 minutes. Transfer pan to rack; cool crust to room temperature, about 30 minutes. Maintain oven temperature.

Place pan with cooled crust on rimmed baking sheet. Using electric mixer, beat cream cheese in large bowl until smooth. Add sugar, flour, lemon peel, and lemon juice; beat until smooth. Add eggs and yolks, one at a time, beating just until incorporated after each addition. Beat in ½ cup sour cream and whipping cream. Pour filling over brownie crust in pan; smooth the top.

Bake cake until puffed, light golden, and set around edges (center will still move slightly when pan is gently shaken), about 1 hour 20 minutes. Remove cake from oven. Maintain oven temperature.

Spoon 1 cup sour cream in dollops over top of cake, then spread evenly over top with offset spatula. Return cake to oven and bake 5 minutes. Run small sharp knife around sides of cake to loosen. Place pan with cake directly in refrigerator and chill uncovered overnight (cake may sink in center). Can be made 2 days ahead. Keep chilled.

When ready to serve, remove pan sides from cake. Run thin sharp knife between pan bottom and crust to loosen. Using 2 metal spatulas as aid, transfer cake to platter. Garnish top edge of cake with chocolate curls and lemon slices.

Chapter 22

THE AMAZING MR. BLOCK

M r. Block showed up at my inn during the horrific ice and snow storms of 2009, which silently stole the power of 177,000 local residents in Louisville. He had his belongings in plastic grocery bags. As he started up the walk, I realized that he might end up flat on his back on the icy pavement, so I sent Ali out to help him.

"Wear your coat when you go out," I warned her. "It's really cold out there."

Christmas had come and gone and it was getting colder by the day. The neighborhood streets were desolate, and many of the houses were without electricity due to downed wires. Fortunately, my side of the street hadn't suffered so far—not that there wasn't still a chance it could.

"Okay, I will," Ali said. "Don't worry, I know how bad it is out there. My car would barely start this morning as I was leaving for work."

Mr. Block was wearing an old red Louisville Cardinals jacket and baggy pants. I could see from the window that he had forgotten his socks and was wearing some old leather bedroom slippers.

Alison helped him up the stairs and he stumbled through the door, spilling his wet plastic bags onto the hardwood floor. He squinted at me through thick, wire-rimmed glasses and stammered out, "I-I-I'm Steven Block. The one who called you about staying with you for a few days because of the storm?"

He was shaking from the cold, and appeared to be somewhat confused. The weather was unusually bad and the winds had taken the chill down to below zero. I figured he probably hadn't eaten much with no electricity. The heavy ice had brought down most of the electrical wires all along the other side of the street.

We had made pumpkin pancakes for breakfast that morning and still had a few left over."How about some pumpkin pancakes for breakfast, Mr. Block?" I asked.

"Yes, pumpkin pancakes would be lovely!"His eyes lit up as he shuffled into the parlor.

He talked for the next ten minutes straight, telling me about the ice storm and how it was ravaging the neighborhood. It had caused the demise of a large tree in his front yeard, and the tree had fallen against his house, damaging it severely. He'd had to leave his icy home, which had no electricity or water, and move to a temporary residence. He went on and on in a series of run-on sentences, repeating himself over and over. He was very distraught.

Ali brought in a cup of hot coffee and escorted Mr. Block into the dining room.

"Just sit here, Mr. Block," she said, gesturing to the little antique table next to the heat register. "I'll get your breakfast ready."

When Ali placed the stack of steaming pancakes and a side dish of bacon in front of him a few minutes later, Mr. Block leaned forward and gave them a little sniff.

"Mmmm, cinnamon," he said. "I love cinnamon."

"And nutmeg. And maple-pecan topping," Ali said.

"Yes," Mr. Block purred. "It looks wonderful."

He gingerly picked up the antique silver fork next to his plate and sliced it through the stack. With a deliberate stick of the fork, he impaled the slice and slowly brought it to his mouth. He savored the bit for a moment, then swallowed it whole and exclaimed, "These are the most delicious pancakes I've ever eaten!" He then proceeded to gobble down the rest, along with the bacon.

I had other guests and a few friends who had called in desperation, looking for a place to stay for a couple of days, occupying rooms already. My heart went out to my local guests, who were reluctant to leave their homes, their pets, and their plants. Like Mr. Block, most of them had thrown a few pieces of clothing and their sundries in plastic bags before making their way to my inn, too cold to go looking for suitcases in their storerooms before leaving in search of warmth and comfort.

When his room was ready, Ali gathered up Mr. Block's plastic bags and told him to follow her. He grabbed hold of the railing and pulled himself up to the second floor step by step. When he got to the top, he stopped to catch his breath and leaned against the wall for a minute before following Ali into his room. We did not hear from him the rest of the night.

The next morning, Mr. Block came down for breakfast early. I was in the kitchen when he peeked in.

"Can't wait for more of those pumpkin pancakes," he chirped.

"Sorry, but today we're having scrambled eggs and cheese," I said as I ushered him into the dining room.

"Oh, that'll be fine," he said. "Will you join me for breakfast?"

He had the forlorn look of a very lonely person. How could I refuse? I smiled. "I'd be happy to."

Seated across from me at the small cherry dining table, Mr. Block proceeded to tell me the story of his life. He began with his major collection of etchings by Picasso, Grant Wood, Currier & Ives, and James Whistler. He said the collection also included a rare Rembrandt etching entitled *Christ before Pilate*.

What? "You have a Rembrandt, Mr. Block?" *This guy has got to be senile.* I was astounded by this revelation, and somewhat skeptical.

"Well," he said through a mouthful of eggs, "the collection is no longer in my possession. I gave it all away."

"You gave it all away?" I asked, still not sure I believed any of it. "Your priceless collection? Why?"

"I don't really care about the money," he said. "They give me a little to tide me over every month. I don't need the money."

"Is it enough to live on?" I asked.

"Along with my pension, I do just fine. I have enough to live on. I don't really need the money," he repeated. "I just didn't want anyone to steal them. They can't steal them there."

"So you gave them to the university?"

"Yes, they are housed in the J.B. Speed Museum at the University of Louisville. They'll be safe there forever. They're at the university," he said, repeating himself again.

All of a sudden, he dropped his fork and headed for the stairs, only to return minutes later with an armful of booklets and brochures.

"The whole story is in these little books," he said, still breathing heavily from the trip up the stairs. And, sure enough, it was all there, with a fine picture of Mr. Block up in the right hand corner. I couldn't believe my eyes.

That evening, I checked in five of my close friends whose homes also had to be evacuated because of the storms. We all gathered in the parlor and were about to have a glass or two of wine when Mr. Block breezed into the room. He was all smiles and had his booklets and brochures with him.

He scurried to the table where he'd had breakfast in the dining room that morning, bent over, and laid out all of his books, brochures, and pictures in a neat row from one side to the other.

He straightened up and turned—too quickly, it seemed, because he stumbled back into the parlor. He stopped in between the pocket doors that connected the parlor and the dining room to catch his balance. Then, facing my friends, he cleared his throat and announced, "Good evening everyone. I am Steven Block, the art collector."

Donna glanced over at me and gave me quizzical look, then looked back at Mr. Block.

"Mr. Block is spending a few days with us," I interjected. "These are my friends, Mr. Block: Valerie and Craig, who are also innkeepers, and Judy, Roger, and Donna."

"I am Steven Block, the art collector," he repeated. "I've come here tonight to talk to you about my priceless collection of art, now hanging at the Speed Art Museum at the University of Louisville—not too far from here—and if you want to see them you can . . ."

"Steven Block?" Craig whispered to me.

"You may stop by the museum and take a look at them whenever you're in the neighborhood," Mr. Block said. He picked up one of his brochures and opened it, holding it up and rotating it from side to side so everyone in the room could see it.

"This is the first group of etchings I gave them. They are hanging in the Speed Art Museum . . . just down the street." He pointed to a picture of an etching by Picasso. Everyone in the room was mesmerized. Seeing that he had a captive audience, Mr. Block walked slowly around the room, bringing the brochure up under the eyes and nose of each person. As he walked toward the other side of the room, Craig leaned over and whispered again, "Is this guy for real? Picasso?"

"He's for real," I said.

"Is this a presentation or something?"

"I don't know," I muttered. "If it is, this is the first time I knew anything about it. I had no idea he was gonna come downstairs and do this."

Mr. Block proceeded to show every one of his brochures to my guests. At first I couldn't believe that he actually intended to give a presentation, but that's what he did, with all the flamboyance of an expert speaker on art collecting.

At first my guests were delighted and interested, but after an hour or so they started losing their enthusiasm. Mr. Block continued talking, repeating half of what he said over and over. The only way to escape from seeing the rest of his materials was for me and my friends to go out to dinner, which we happily did despite the wintry weather.

The next evening, and every evening after that while he was a guest at Aleksander House, Mr. Block joined us in the parlor, entertaining my friends and interjecting himself into our conversation with stories about his collections and pictures in catalogs, which he held up over his head for all to see in a kind of "show and tell" demonstration.

It became more and more apparent as time went on that his memory was affected by his age. In some ways he was annoying, but he was also charming, informative, and brilliant. Yes, he had been a collector, but, as I spent more time with him, I discovered that his collecting days had been over for many years, and had only come about in the first place by happenstance. Collecting was never his primary profession.

Mr. Block, it turned out, had earned his undergraduate degree in sociology before going off to Harvard grad school to study community planning. After working on a city planning project in Italy for two years, he ended up in Washington DC, where he stayed for forty years, designing and implementing a nationwide community service program by the name of Vista (now known as AmericaCorps VISTA). He returned to Louisville in 2004, when he was seventy years old, and bought a house three blocks from my bed and breakfast in Old Louisville.

Mr. Block spent an entire week with me. When his home was ready for his return, he packed up his things in his plastic bags and checked out. He left me articles and a Whistler catalog naming all the thirty-odd etchings he had donated to the university.

I watched Mr. Block walk away from my second floor window where I could hear the *shhhh*ing sound of huge branches falling from my beautiful magnolia tree; the branches, still heavily laden with ice and snow, were falling one by one across the icy front walk leading to the house. I was thankful that I was away from the storm, warm, cozy, and quiet in my beautiful Victorian home.

Pumpkin Pancakes (Mr. Block's favorites)

Ingredients
2 eggs
1 cup buttermilk
½ cup pureed pumpkin
2 cups pancake mix
4 tablespoons butter, melted
1 teaspoon cinnamon
½ teaspoon nutmeg

Instructions
Beat eggs and buttermilk together with a whisk. Add pureed pumpkin and beat well. Add two cups of pancake mix, one at a time, with more milk if necessary. Add spices and melted butter. Whisk together into a smooth, thick batter. Spoon one ladle full for each of eight pancakes onto an electric grill. When pancakes begin to form little holes, turn and lightly brown. Do not turn more than once. Serve with maple-pecan sauce.

MAPLE-PECAN SAUCE

Instructions
Mix together 1 cup maple syrup, 2 tablespoons butter, and a hand-full of chopped pecans. Boil until syrup is slightly reduced. To serve, place one tablespoon of butter onto the top of each layer of a stack of three pancakes. Pour the hot sauce over the top.

Chapter 23

KARI

By April of 2009, Ali had gotten a full-time job as a chef and I began looking for another housekeeper. Again, I posted an ad in the culinary department of Sullivan University. I was anxious to get someone trained by the time the Mid-America Trucking Show rolled around in March.

When Kari came to interview for the job, I liked her right away. She was personable, attractive, and smart. And from the very beginning, she told me her dream was to be an innkeeper. She loved my bed and breakfast and wanted it for her own.

If Kari and her husband had had the money for a down payment, I would have sold it to them right then, lock, stock, and barrel. But that wasn't the case. I did hire her, however, and I hired another girl Sandra, too, for part-time work. I knew I would need all the help I could get when Derby rolled around.

Kari had been working for me for some time when I began noticing a few peculiarities. She had a way of "standing at attention" whenever I pointed something out that she'd forgotten to do or wasn't doing right. Occasionally, she would click her heels like Dorothy in *The Wizard of Oz* before doing it. I figured it was a carryover from a very strict upbringing.

Kari also exhibited a variety of facial tics and expressions. And whenever I asked her to make some cookies or muffins, she would clap her hands and jump up and down in a state of glee. She was almost childlike at times—especially in her knack for destroying things. She was always taking things apart and then failing to get them back together again. She did it with my electric can opener, the microwave, and the alarm clock in one of the guest rooms. She was really good at destroying things. I had numbers on the knobs of my stove—but not for long after she started working for me.

She was, however, a clean freak—perfect for someone working in a bed and breakfast. She loved to clean the bathrooms and appliances. That was how I lost the numbers on the knobs of my stove, actually: she just kept scrubbing and scrubbing until she scrubbed all the numbers right off. I freaked out and laid into her about it, so she drew three black circles on the oven knob with an indelible pen: one for 250, one for 350, and one for 450.

The next day, in her continued cleaning frenzy, she scrubbed the circles off again, without even noticing, and forgot to tell me before she left. Have you ever tried to heat your oven to350 degrees with an oven knob that has no numbers? I was burning everything. I put a couple of slices of pizza in for dinner and moved the knob to where I thought 350 was and set the timer—and when I opened the oven door, smoke poured out. Little black slices of pepperoni stared up at me from the shriveled triangles.

I was so mad I lost my appetite. I ran to my laptop and e-mailed Kari a scathing description of what had happened, beseeching her to return the next day and draw on some more circles.

One day, Kari and I decided to shampoo the carpet and furniture in one of the guest rooms. Before we got started, we had to move a humongous glass coffee table into the adjoining room. I leaned the glass from the top of the table against the loveseat so it wouldn't get broken—but for some reason Kari pushed against the other end of the loveseat after I let go, and the glass started to fall. We both ran to catch it.

We succeeded in saving the glass. *Crisis averted*, I thought.

But the loveseat was too near the doorway now.

"I've got it," Kari said, and she pushed it back the other way with one big hard shove. The sofa slammed against my beautiful Grecian floor lamp, shattering the white porcelain shade and denting the lamp base—another thing to add to the long list of things she had broken or destroyed.

I was so upset I sent her into the other room to shampoo the white sofa there. But when I walked into the room, she wasn't shampooing at all; she was taking the stuffing out of one of the bolster covers.

"What are you doing, Kari? I told you *not* to take the stuffing out of the bolster covers. You'll never get it all back in right."

"But I thought the bolster covers needed to be washed."

"We cannot wash them separately from the rest of the sofa. If you wash them in the machine, they'll be a different color from the rest of the sofa. They won't match."

"But they're all white," she said.

"I know, Kari, but there are lots of shades of white."

"There are? I just thought white was white."

She quickly stuffed the bolster back into the cover, cotton batten and all. Of course it didn't go back in smoothly. It never was the same. It was all crumpled and rippled-looking along the top where it had been smooth before. It certainly didn't match the other one.

I got in the habit of checking the rooms that she said she'd completed and made ready for check-in after she left for the day. There was *always* something undone, done wrong, not finished, or missing. She would forget one of the drinking glasses or robes. She would leave the Windex bottle or a large roll of paper towels in the middle of the room. A pillow case might be missing from one of the pillows, or she'd mix up the five towels we placed in the room and put two different kinds of towels on the rack that didn't match.

She took window shades down and put them back up backwards. She left laundry in the washer and dryer and dishes in the dishwasher after I told her not to. She burned dozens of muffins and cookies, and broke dishes, glasses, an electric can opener, and a waffle iron. And she always came to work late. But she was very bright, so I imagined how very frustrating it must be for her to keep making mistakes and forgetting all the time, and I always forgave her. She kept trying, after all, and she had a good spirit. I really admired that about her. And my guests loved her.

By this time, I was in my late seventies and running the business was becoming difficult for me. There were three flights of stairs in the house and my arthritis had been getting worse. Kari and I talked often about she and her husband buying my inn. She was anxious to learn the business, so I thought that if I trained her to do everything she could manage the business for me. I spent hours training her. She had been with me almost two years at that point. She had improved her cleaning skills and had a handle on the day-to-day operations; she just needed to learn the financial part of it, and how to price and conduct special parties and events.

One afternoon a woman who Kari said sounded like a lovely southern lady called about throwing a Victorian tea party for her four-year-old granddaughter. She wanted to rent the entire first floor for the event.

I didn't usually do Victorian tea parties; they were too time-consuming and work-intensive, and cost more than most people wanted to pay.

But Kari begged me to take on the event. "Nancy, I really want to do this," she said. "I'm trying to learn the business, and this is one thing I will be doing a lot of when I buy the inn from you."

"I know, Kari," I said, "but I just don't have the time to put into the planning and serving. And moneywise, it's not worth the trouble."

"You don't have to do anything," she insisted. "I'll do it all. And the woman said she didn't care how much it cost."

I thought about it overnight and decided to go ahead and let her do it. But I was staying clear of the whole thing. I had promised Kari would train her before I moved to Austin, and this would be a good opportunity for her to learn to plan and execute parties, as well as how to work closely with guests. I knew she would have a thousand questions, and I didn't want her calling me in Austin after I left.

Picturing a small gathering of little girls in the dining room, I thought Kari could do it. How much time could it take? And how hard could it be to make a few tiny sandwiches and teacakes?

"Okay, Kari," I said the next day, "why don't you come up with some ideas for the menu and let me see them. We can work out the costs so you can let her know what they'll be."

Kari carefully worked out the menu—mostly little tea sandwiches and teacakes. And tea, of course. I told her to be sure and figure out what ingredients she would need to make each item and to find out the costs of each one. Everything should be noted and accounted for, right down to the last teabag.

"You have to factor in all the food costs, plus the time it will take to shop, make everything, set up, serve, and clean up," I told her. "It's a lot of work."

"I know, I know. But I think it'll be fun." She was ecstatic.

Mrs. DeRiley was delighted when Kari told her she would manage the event. It was the first time Kari had ever done anything like this and I was anxious to see if she could handle it. She e-mailed Mrs. DeRiley the menu and the fun began.

At seven o'clock that night, Mrs. DeRiley called the bed and breakfast. She had received the menu and wanted to discuss it. I told her Kari was handling the party and wouldn't be there until the next day. She hung up and I went back to eating my dinner.

At seven thirty, the phone rang again. When I answered it, Mrs. DeRiley started in about the menu:

"Mrs. Hinchliff, I just want to make sure Kari knows what she's doing. I want this party to be perfect for my little Sara. She's such a dear, sweet thing. Kari has on the menu tuna and egg salad tea sandwiches, but Sara doesn't like eggs."

"Mrs. DeRiley, you'll have to talk to Kari about that," I said. "She'll be here tomorrow."

"Well, I just wanted to check with you to see if the pricing was right."

"Yes it is, Mrs. DeRiley, I went over it with her."

"Okay then, I will call tomorrow."

At 8 P.M., the phone rang again. This time I didn't answer it. But when I checked my voicemail, sure enough, it was Mrs. DeRiley again. I could see the writing on the wall.

I called Kari.

"Mrs. DeRiley's been calling me all night," I told her. "Did you give her your phone number?"

"No," Kari said. "Should I?"

"Yes," I said, "you have to call her and give it to her. I cannot field all these calls, Kari."

The next day Kari called and worked out the sandwich changes with Mrs. DeRiley, who also wanted to make sure there were going to be brownies, which were Sara's favorite.

"And, Kari, could we please have some of those little petit fours? I prefer homemade ones. You do know how to make them, right?"

No, Kari didn't know how to make them. But she was going to learn.

In the ensuing days, Mrs. DeRiley kept changing the plans. She started by adding more people and activities. All the while, she was insisting that Kari was not getting it right. At the beginning, there was to be only one adult, who would pour the tea from the huge silver urn. Now there would be four. My dining room was not that large, so already it would be a little crowded—and, of course, this increased the amount of food and drink Kari had to prepare, taking the price up.

"Sara likes orange, so maybe some kind of orange-flavored tea would be good," Mrs. DeRiley said. "And the adults like jasmine or oolong. You are using the very best teas, right? From Taiwan?"

Kari had this conversation with her at ten P.M., when she was home with her family.

Mrs. DeRiley insisted on calling several times a day, every day. I thought this would be a good lesson in problem solving and placating guests for Kari. However, she did not know how to control the situation, so Mrs. DeRiley kept leading her around in all directions, changing things and then going back to the original ideas. And the request about making petit fours? I told Kari making them was out of the question. She didn't know how, and they were pretty tricky to make. If Mrs. DeRiley wanted to pay extra, Kari could order some from the corner bakery for the party, but she wasn't going to waste her time trying to do it herself.

By the third day, Mrs. DeRiley had talked Kari into hiring a friend to dress up like Cinderella. She wanted Kari to go out in search of a Cinderella costume, magic wand and all.

"I will pay for it, of course," she said. "Money is no object when it comes to Sara. She is the dearest, sweetest child . . . my only grandchild."

Next, she convinced Kari to hire a horse-drawn coach with footmen, again in costume, to pick the children up and bring them to the door.

Kari was having a hard time keeping up with everything. She frequently called Mrs. DeRiley to report and check with her on whether the plans were as she expected, but Mrs. DeRiley wouldn't call her back for days—and by the time she did, she would have forgotten what she had asked for in the first place and blame it on Kari. By the sixth day, Kari announced to me there would be somewhere between sixteen and twenty people coming, and they would be gathering in the parlor. She knew I wouldn't like that. Mrs. DeRiley hadn't reserved the parlor, and I didn't want to rent it to her.

"All those kids trampling on my newly-shampooed oriental carpet?" I said. "No way. Absolutely not."

When Kari heard this, she collapsed onto the sofa, looking like she was about to have a nervous breakdown. "But I promised her."

"Without asking me?" I shook my head. "You'll have to figure something else out, Kari."

The final straw was when Mrs. DeRiley announced she wanted the media there so they could do a big story on the event. I balked. I did not want the publicity. An argument between Kari and Mrs. DeRiley ensued, and Mrs. DeRiley started getting pretty nasty with Kari.

Up to this point I had kept pretty much out of the whole thing, but when Kari told me what Mrs. DeRiley had said to her on the phone, I decided to intercede. I called her immediately.

"Mrs. DeRiley, this is Nancy, the owner of Aleksander House. I need to talk with you about the tea party. Kari will no longer be working with you. I've taken her off the booking. And I really must tell you that I do not like the way you have been treating her."

"Me?" Mrs. DeRiley sputtered. "It's *her* who is not treating *me* right. She keeps getting everything all mixed up, and she doesn't know how to cater."

"What do you mean she doesn't know how to cater?"

"Well, she told me she didn't know how to make petit fours. And—"

"Mrs. DeRiley, Kari is bending over backwards to accommodate you," I said. "But it's no wonder she's confused; you keep changing the format and the food and telling her she's doing everything wrong. Then you ask her to search for and buy a Cinderella costume and wear it to the party, or to get one of her friends to do it. That wasn't in the original agreement."

"But—"

"And the carriage to pick up the girls?" I interjected. I wasn't done yet. "You never said anything about that at the beginning."

"Well, I just thought of it," Mrs. DeRiley said.

"And the publicity?" I continued. "I do not want any publicity. I don't want the media here."

"Why not?" She sounded shocked. "It would be good advertising for your inn."

"I don't need any advertising, Mrs. DeRiley. And when I do, I'll decide what kind."

I didn't feel I owed this woman an explanation. But the fact was, business was good even without the advertising—and I was trying to cut back a bit. I was already in negotiations to sell the inn to Kari and her husband, and I was all tied up with packing, figuring out how to move my furniture and car to Austin, and making plans with my daughter to buy a house. Besides, I didn't like the idea of creating a huge event at my house that could potentially turn into a fiasco.

"Well," Mrs. DeRiley said, "I find that very strange. What kind of place are you running, anyhow? Why don't you want more business?"

She would not back down on the publicity issue. But neither would I.

"Mrs. DeRiley," I finally said, "I really don't think we can work things out here. I'm sorry, but I will have to cancel the whole party."

"You what?" she screamed. "You can't do that."

"I just did."

I hung up the phone and waited for it to start ringing off the hook. I knew she would call back. When she did, I shut down all three phones, went into my room, sat down, and turned on the TV.

The day after that final conversation with Mrs. DeRiley, we started getting calls from her daughters, all of them threatening to go to their lawyers. One of her daughters *was* a lawyer, in fact—something she was quick to inform me of when she called. They used every trick in the book to dissuade me. When that didn't work, Mrs. DeRiley called again and left a message.

"We're from one of the finest and most prominent families in Louisville," she said. "My husband is a judge and I am a professor. All of my children graduated from the finest universities . . ." She went on and on. "You can't do this to me."

Well, sorry, Mrs. DeRiley, but I did. And I didn't regret it for a minute.

Recipes

Tea sandwiches

Tomato-Cheddar: Spread mayonnaise on white bread. Sandwich with sliced tomato, aged cheddar and watercress. Trim the crusts and cut into pieces.

Ham, Brie and Apple: Spread softened butter and Dijon mustard inside a split loaf of French bread. Fill with deli ham, sliced Brie and sliced green apple. Cut into pieces.

Cucumber-Butter: Mix 4 tablespoons softened butter, ½ teaspoon grated lemon zest and 1 tablespoon chopped fresh herbs. Spread on white bread and sandwich with sliced cucumber. Trim the crusts and cut into pieces.

Watercress-Butter: Make Cucumber-Butter sandwiches as above, but fill with watercress instead of cucumber.

Chapter 24

SELLING MY INN

I'd been trying to sell my house for a while, but the housing market was bad and it wasn't selling, so I came up with an idea for Kari and her husband to buy it on a land contract. They loved the idea, and I knew how much they wanted it and would do everything in their power to make it happen. But six months went by and they still had not made a firm offer of any kind. I hoped that everything would work out, because I was ready to reinvent myself again . . . this time as a writer. And I couldn't do that while running the inn.

First they'd say they were putting their house up for sale; then they'd change their minds and decide to do a little rehab and staging—change the paint in the kitchen, put in new flooring (the old flooring had been ruined when the water flowed out from the *back* of the machine because Kari took it apart while it was still full), and put in a new tub. Each thing took forever to finish. It took Marty three or four days just to put the tub in. I think he miscalculated the size of it or something.

Finally, Kari and Marti decided they definitely wanted to buy my bed and breakfast on a land contract, but first they needed to sell their own house. So they went about trying to sell it themselves. Meanwhile, Kari asked me to continue teaching her the business so she and her husband could buy it, along with the house. I agreed, of course. She already knew most of the day-to-day operation. Now I just had to teach her the financial part.

Kari and Marti finally put their house up for sale on Craigslist and put a sign out in front. *Good start*, I thought. But unfortunately that's all they did, except for talking to Marti's seventy-eight-year-old ex-realtor grandmother, who told them not to advertise in the paper because ads were too expensive nowadays. So they waited for two months while I fretted.

"Are you getting any bites?" I kept asking Kari.

"Well, three people walked by today and slowed down to read the sign."

"Why don't you get a realtor?"

"Oh no, we can do this ourselves."

It took them two or three weeks to get pictures up on Craigslist, and even then all they put up was a picture of the living room (good), the dining room (good), one small bedroom with a dilapidated twin bed covered in a faded satin comforter (bad), and the sink in their tiny bathroom (very bad). Kari told me they were going to link to a page with more pictures of the kitchen, garden, master bedroom and master bath, but when Marti, the procrastinator, finally did put up a link, it didn't work.

Needless to say, I was pulling my hair out with frustration. I didn't want to move forward with selling them my house until I was sure they would sell theirs. They had been dragging their feet since last summer, when they'd first showed an interest in becoming innkeepers. I had doubted it would happen then, and I doubted that it would happen now.

I continued to ask Kari her how the house sale was going every day when she showed up to work.

"No action yet," she'd reply with a smile.

She didn't seem the least bit concerned that only three people had inquired in almost two months. Finally, after weeks of absolutely nothing happening, I suggested again that they get a realtor. "Oh no," Kari protested. "We can't afford a realtor."

They had priced their house rather low, and they needed to come out with enough cash to purchase my bed and breakfast outright—that was the deal. After that, they could move into the inn, and they would have three years to buy it on a land contract (or lease to rent, as it is sometimes called). In the meantime I planned on moving to Austin so I could be near my daughter.

I really thought they could get more for their house than they were asking. It was small, but it was a charmer—a three-bedroom in a cul-de-sac in an excellent neighborhood. And it was in great shape.

Finally, they saw the light. After wasting two months waiting alone every weekend for no one to come and buy their house, they got a realtor. After signing them up, the guy put pictures of their house online and made a real effort to ensure the deal was done before the April 30th first-time buyer incentive cutoff.

The house sold within a week. What a professional! Who knew? Certainly not Kari and Marti. And he had even raised the asking price so they would have the money to buy my bed and breakfast.

Although I was somewhat worried about the ability of these two thirty-year-olds to run a bed and breakfast, I was still willing to go along with it. And since Kari and Marti had the cash they needed now, the next thing was to work out separate contracts with my real estate lawyer for selling both the business and my house.

We started mapping the property contract. We changed it many times along the way—it started out as a "Lease to Buy" and ended up as a "Bond For Purchase," or land contract, the actual name varies with different states—but eventually we figured out something that worked for everyone.

Next I spent an entire week in Austin looking for a house. By the end of the week, I had found two houses that were very affordable. With my daughter's help, I decided on a beautiful four-bedroom ranch-type house in a lovely neighborhood in Georgetown, a suburb of Austin. It was farther away from my daughter than I would have liked, but it was a great house, and absolutely perfect for me and my furniture.

I was very excited thinking about the move and the new house. I'd wanted to move for the past five years, and now it looked like it was really going to happen. I had everything in place: a moving company had been retained, my new house had been purchased, and everything I was taking with me was packed. All I had to do now was sell a few pieces of furniture I didn't need, deposit the check I was going to get from Kari and Marti when I returned to Louisville, make my flight arrangements, and get someone to drive my car to Austin. I was nervous as hell, but very happy.

The next morning, I jumped out of bed and ran downstairs to make that all-important pot of freshly ground brew. Then I raced back upstairs to check out my e-mail. I knew Kari and Marti had news about the closing, and I was dying to see when I could be expecting the check for the sale of the business. When I got it, I'd be able to send Chris the money I needed for the down payment on my new house. I was so excited.

As I clicked on my mail inbox, the first thing I saw was an e-mail from Marti:

Sent: Monday, June 28, 2010 8:50 PM
We will meet you at 2 P.M. for the signing of the Land Contract.

I was ecstatic.

But my excitement was short-lived, because then I read Marti's next e-mail, from the following day:

Sent: Tuesday, Jun 29, 2010 at 6:21 PM
Nancy,
After closing, the total amount paid to us was
substantially lower than we had anticipated. Our
mortgage company added a significant amount to
our principal balance in attorney fees and back due
interest that no one had bothered to tell us about.
We cleared just over $18,000.00. We are going to
contact our bankruptcy trustee to see if there is some
mistake, but it does not look promising. With this new
figure, we do not see any possibility of purchasing the
business. I realize that this is not how anyone wanted
this to turn out. For all this work and time both sides
have put in to have come to nothing is unfortunate,
but we have exhausted our options . . .
—Kari and Marti

What? How could they have no idea they would only come out with $18,000 after the sale of their house? How could they ever think they could pay for my business? The asking price was $50,000 cash. Where were they going to get the rest of it? They had borrowed $10,000 from Kari's mom, so they had $28,000 altogether . . . but that still wasn't close to enough to buy the business. The deal was off!

Well, it's over now, I thought. *They don't have the money . . . no big surprise there.*

Somewhere in my psyche, bells had been going off the whole time we were negotiating. I had plenty of reason to doubt that the deal would ever come to fruition, but, cock-eyed optimist that I am, I went along with it, thinking it would eventually work out. Actually, it was more than optimism—it was my strong desire to get out of a business that had become too strenuous for me to handle at my age. That was what had kept me believing, or at least hoping, that the deal would happen.

Anyhow, it didn't, so I was now back to "going with the flow" again. I put my house up for sale again and started working with a great realtor friend of mine to make a sale as soon as possible.

I really didn't have a lot of anger toward Kari, because I knew how much she'd wanted this and how hard she and her husband worked to make it happen. They'd even sold their house. She worked for me for a couple more weeks after the deal fell through, but soon gave her notice; she needed to take a full-time job so she and Marti could save some money and put their lives back together. They stayed with friends and family for a while until they could rent a house. All of their belongings were in storage till then, so their family of four (they had two young boys) was in upheaval. They had lost their house, the deposit on my house, and the difference between $18,000 and $60,000.

She was homeless and without a full-time job. But that was her problem. I had problems of my own. I had to get my brain to start focusing on my business again.

I was disappointed by this turn of events, yes, but life goes on—and as I said, I decided to just with go the flow. I think my daughter in Austin was more upset than I was. For my own part, I knew I would eventually get to Austin. For now I simply had to delay the inevitable. The work was hard on me physically, but I knew that if I got a good assistant I'd be just fine.

I got through that next year like I always do when I'm confronted with a crisis: one step at a time. Life went on, the bed and breakfast went on, and my dream of moving to Austin went flying out the window. I did not unpack a thing; I just started all over again. When winter came, I bought a new scarf, hat, mittens, and boots. I wasn't about to scramble through the forty boxes that were ready to go to Austin, some of them unlabeled.

I ended up keeping Sandra on rather than hiring someone new, and it turned out she was easier to work with than Kari. She made fewer mistakes and had an unusually good memory.

It would be a year before I realized how very disappointing

the whole thing had been. That's when all the anger came out. But with the help of my psychotherapist daughter, Kristi, I got through that too.

I was so glad to see Kari and winter go, and when warmer weather arrived in 2010, it was time to think about spring and summer dishes. I was getting a lot of visitors who were on special diets. It seemed the whole world was becoming gluten-free. We occasionally did light suppers for groups of businesspeople, and that year one of the favorite items on our menu was a salad my daughter concocted.

Spring Salad with Mango and Goat Cheese
(Serves 4)

SALAD

Ingredients
1 cup spring greens
1 yellow bell pepper, chopped
1 cup grape tomatoes, halved
½ cup shredded carrots
2-3 green onion sprigs, sliced
1 cup chopped mango
2 baked, roasted, or fried chicken breasts, cut into bite-sized pieces
1 small avocado, chopped and sprinkled with lime juice

DRESSING

Ingredients
1¼ cups olive oil
Juice of 1½ limes
1 tablespoon wine vinegar
Fresh basil, chopped
½ cup Thai Chili Garlic Sauce (check your local gourmet food market)
Goat cheese, crumbled

Instructions
Lightly toss first six ingredients together, except for avocado, in a large salad bowl. Add chicken and gently mix.

Combine remaining ingredients, except for goat cheese, in a small jar and shake to mix thoroughly.

Pour dressing over vegetables and toss thoroughly. Add avocado.

To serve, ladle onto salad plates and top with crumbled goat cheese.

Chapter 25

JASONSPEAK

I continued to rely heavily on Sullivan University's Culinary Arts School for employees over the years. One of the last few years I was in business, right after the sale of the house and business fell though, and Kari and I had agreed it would be best if she left, things seemed to have gotten somewhat back to normal and Sandra had agreed to work full-time.

Sandra was a chefing major and had two little children, so she was good in the kitchen as well as with the housework. I was delighted that she decided to stay after Kari left. But she had only been working for me about a year when she announced to me one day that she had to take some time off.

"I'm pregnant," she said, tears edging their way down her flushed cheeks.

"You're what?"

"I know . . . I know." Her voice was small and apologetic.

"Sandra, you have two kids under three right now. And you're a single mom. What are you going to do with a third one?"

"I don't know," she said, groaning.

Of course, I was not just concerned about her and how she and her deadbeat husband were going to afford another kid; the thought of looking for more help made me queasy. It wasn't an easy process. And most of the students from the Culinary Arts School couldn't stay with me for more than a year or two, since graduation just kept rolling around and claiming them. I was constantly interviewing and training new people.

One of the biggest problems I had was finding someone whose personality and work ethic would mesh with mine. I am a perfectionist, and I ran my business like a drill sergeant. I had to have someone who could cook and clean, and who was as detail-oriented as I was. They needed to be somewhat laid-back and able to tolerate work-intensive periods that sometimes lasted up to five or six days in a row. And, of course, they had to deal with me . . . not easy. It took me months to train someone to carry out the operation as I would and get them to a place where I could stay on the computer and write while they carried on in the kitchen and guest rooms.

Sandra had gotten to that place. But now what?

"My mom is going to kill me," she said.

"Why?" I asked, although I had a pretty good idea. Sandra's mother was very supportive; she helped with the kids, and occasionally came up with an extra hundred or so here and there to give to Sandra. She might see this new development as more work and money out of her pocket. I knew from what Sandra told me that she was also hoping Sandra would divorce Jack, who was always out of work and was becoming increasingly abusive.

"She doesn't want me to have more kids now," Sandra said.

"Well, it's too late for that now," I said. I was too upset about the news to be sympathetic. "What are you going to do?"

"I'm gonna have it," she said. "I want more kids anyhow. I've always wanted three or four."

"Okay," I said, "so what about work?" No beating around the bush here . . . I had to know.

"You can put up another notice at the University, hire another person, and I'll train them before I get to my ninth month."

And so the search was on. I e-mailed my notice for more help to the school, and it didn't take long for calls to start coming in. There was no problem getting responses; the problem would come later, when I began the interview process.

After seventeen years, I had gotten pretty good at screening applicants. My first interview was always on the phone. I could usually narrow down the applicants to four or five rather quickly. These I would have come to the bed and breakfast for a more in-depth conversation.

I usually hired women, although I had hired two young men in the past. Women seemed to know more about housework, laundry, shopping for groceries and supplies, and general organization of a household. However, this time most of my respondents were young men—so, after a couple of interviews, I narrowed it down to two, Darien and Jason. I brought them both in for a day to see how they would work out, and ended up hiring Jason.

Jason was an out-of-work musician who had studied photography in college. He'd met his wife there while both were working on art degrees. He was laid-back and seemed like he would be able to work well with both me and Sandra.

Sandra was mostly in charge of training Jason, but I had to take over on the days she wasn't there and make sure his training continued. It usually took me six months to a year to fully train someone who had never worked in a bed and breakfast or hotel before. It is very detail-oriented work and takes time to master.

With the cooking, for example, it wasn't just a matter of telling my new employees to go in the kitchen and make some scrambled eggs with cheese, toast, and bacon. There was so much more to it. We created dishes that were very sophisticated and work-intensive—omelets, quiches, frittatas, Grand Marnier French toast, and pears poached in white Zinfandel—and the cooking itself was only a small part of the food operation. There was also serving, setting up the dining room properly, creating menus, grocery shopping and selection, performing cleanup, storing the food, etc. Food storage, for instance, was extremely important; how you stored it and where could affect the length of time it stayed edible.

This also went for supplies. Can you imagine everyone running around looking for the toilet bowl cleaner because someone put it back in the wrong place? Or leaving Kleenex off the supply shopping list? Next time we needed a box, there wouldn't be any.

Unfortunately, that's what started to happen with Jason. He simply couldn't remember where everything went and, although instructed time and again to put whatever we were running out of on the shopping list (which was pinned to the refrigerator with a magnet, in plain sight), he constantly forgot to do so. This went on seemingly forever, even after he'd been working at my inn for seven weeks.

Keeping everything restocked and refilled appeared to be too much for Jason. He just couldn't remember to do it. He'd fill a sugar bowl or put an extra roll of toilet paper and the hand soap in one of the bathrooms, but forget the other bathrooms. He'd forget the teas in the dining room, the coffee beans, and on and on, till it drove me crazy. I had to go after him every time he was there and check his work, especially the refills. I made suggestions, like keeping a list, focusing on the job at hand, putting himself in the guest's place and asking himself what they would need—but all to no avail.

Sandra or I would go to the linen closet to get sheets for one of the rooms and often discover they weren't there. After searching all the storage areas, we'd find them in the wrong place, or still in the washer or dryer. Or we'd be out of toilet bowl cleaner or creamers or couldn't find the right spatula or whisk or knife. After a few weeks of this, I was starting to climb the walls. Was he ever going to "get it"?

I began pointing out the importance of organization every

time I worked with Jason, emphasizing that when there was more than one person working in the same place, there had to be specific places where every single thing was kept. You would think he would get it, especially after all the times we had to call him on the phone and ask where the skinny metal spatula with the worn-out yellow handle that I'd had for thirty-five years was.

This mediating process became all-consuming—and after Jason had been with us for seven weeks, I started losing patience and began nagging him. I had never been a nagger before, but I caught on to it real fast when logical discussion and suggestions for remembering didn't work. It got so that every time Jason was at the inn I spent at least an hour nagging and pointing out what he was doing wrong. I hated it. I was becoming the wicked witch of the Midwest. Plus, I knew this method usually didn't work with most people, and I fully expected him to just walk out one day. I was escalating with every new event, and becoming more and more abusive. I felt guilty and frustrated, and I thought of firing him many times—but Sandra was pregnant, and I didn't want to go through the process of interviewing and hiring someone else again.

One day I noticed that a small pillow I kept on one of the beds on the third floor was missing.

"Jason, where's the pillow in room number four?"

"What pillow?" He looked confused.

"The little red, green, and black one I made seventeen years ago when I opened the bed and breakfast. I told you about it before, remember?"

He shrugged. "I have no idea."

"Do you remember seeing it?"

"I've never seen it."

"What?" I almost shouted. "How could you never have seen it? It's always on the bed."

He'd been working at the inn for weeks, making that bed every time he was there. I couldn't believe that he didn't know what pillow I was talking about. But he just stood there, like he always did when confronted with the obvious, and looked at me with his now infamous blank stare.

"I'll look for it," he finally said. But he always said that when something was missing. And he could never find it.

Three days later, I noticed a blanket throw was missing from room #3 on the second floor. Again, I asked Jason where it was. He said he didn't know what I was talking about but would look for it.

Did he find it? Not a chance.

Other things went missing from time to time, and when I asked Jason about them, he wouldn't even remember having ever seen them. I started worrying he was drinking or on drugs. What else could explain the gaps in his memory? I was convinced he was holed up in his tiny apartment smoking pot every night and that it was affecting his brain.

One day a man from AAA came to inspect my bed and breakfast. If we were approved, we would be listed in the AAA travel guide. He'd been to the inn before, and always swiped the tops of the pictures hanging on the wall and got down on his knees in the guest rooms and checked for dust bunnies under the bed as part of his inspection.

He came downstairs when he was done.

"How did we do?" I asked.

"There was a lot of dust under the bed in room number four," he said."And a small pillow."

"What?" This really upset me; I had told Jason over and over to make sure he dusted under the bed, but obviously it hadn't made an impression on him. And the pillow? He certainly would have seen it if he'd been dusting.

When the AAA man was gone, I found Jason and told him about the feedback."Did you check out the whole room thoroughly and dust under the bed?" I demanded.

"Of course . . . I always do that," he answered, looking me straight in the eye like I was some kind of crazy person to ask such a ridiculous question.

But now that I knew where the pillow was, I was determined to find the throw. I e-mailed one of the guests who had stayed in room before the throw disappeared and asked if anyone in her party had seen it. She e-mailed me back almost immediately and told me one of the girls had stuffed it under the mattress of the rollaway she'd slept on to lift her head up a bit.

"Sorry, we forgot to tell you," she wrote.

You're sorry! I thought. *You have no idea how sorry I am.*

So the AAA man had found the missing pillow and I had found the throw. Why did I need Jason? Oh yes, to take out the garbage, scrub the kitchen floor, and make the beds . . . all the things that were hard for me and pregnant Sandra to do. But now we were not only doing our jobs, we were doing his too.

After receiving the e-mail about the throw, I asked Jason about it again.

"I scoured the room thoroughly and couldn't find it," he told me.

"Did you look inside the rollaway?" I asked.

"Yes," he said, "I even put new sheets and pillow cases on it."

"Jason, did you look under the mattress?"

"Yes, of course."

Oh yes, of course, I thought, biting my tongue.

I had gotten to the point where I refused to give him the information he needed to solve whatever problem loomed before him. And this one was really looming. I did this not to torture him—although I contemplated doing so more than once—but to get him to think and learn to problem-solve for himself. It was the teacher in me that made me do it, not the devil. Problem solving was extremely important in our business.

I'll be damned if I tell him where the pillow and the throw are, I thought. *He's gonna have to figure it out on his own.*

Having a conversation with Jason was like pulling teeth. When he talked to me, he always added superfluous information so that by the time he got to the end of the sentence, I had no idea what the subject was. The worst part, though, was the response I got when I asked him a direct question. Sometimes he just stood there with a blank expression on his face, saying nothing, like he was in a trance or something and I wasn't even there. Other times, he answered your question with totally unrelated information. For example:

Question: *"Jason, why is this sponge always so dirty?"*
Jason's answer: *"It's coming apart. I have to get a new one."*
Correct answer: *"Because I wipe up stuff I've spilled on the floor with it."*

After a few responses like this, I had to ask the original question again to break down his responses and try to figure out what he meant. Since I was familiar with learning disabilities, emotional and behavior disorders, and various types of cognitive dysfunction from my years as a teacher, that's the first place my mind went for answers to why this kept happening. That and the pot, that is.

Sandra, who was more patient than I was, also started becoming annoyed because half the time she couldn't find anything and the other half of time she couldn't understand Jason. We started referring to his style of conversing as "Jasonspeak."

One day I made a list of the work I wanted Jason to do and put it in order of what to do first, second, etc. He was to do room #2, and then room #3. I handed him the list and sent him off.

When fifteen minutes had passed and I didn't hear Jason in #2, I went to see what was going on. The room wasn't finished, and he was nowhere to be found. I walked into the back hall where #1—the room I was staying in—was, and saw that he had propped open my door. I had not asked him to go into my room, so I was perplexed and irritated.

I could hear him down on the first floor, so I leaned over the banister and called for him to come back up. He came running.

"Why did you go in my room and leave the door propped open?" I asked. "Anyone could walk in there, and my purse is just sitting out in plain sight!"

"I went in there to get the towels out of the bathroom," he said.

"Why? I'm still using them."

"So I could clean the room."

"But why were you going to clean my room? It's not on the list." *God, what is wrong with him?* "Jason," I said slowly, "go down and get my towels."

"Okay." He nodded and ran back downstairs. But when nearly five minutes passed and he didn't come back, I headed back down to the kitchen, sore knees and all, to see what he was doing. And there he was . . . doing something totally unrelated to the problem at hand. He had started a new task: he was pulling all the dirty laundry out of the basket and throwing everything into the washer.

"What are you doing?" I asked. "Where are my towels? Did you check the list?"

"Yes."

"What does it say?"

"It says to clean room number two first, then number three."

"Does it say to clean my room?"

"No."

"Then why did you prop open the door to my room and take out the towels?"

"I thought I should do the whole second floor."

"Where did you ever get that idea?"

"I just thought . . . "

I didn't even hear his response. *Please don't think, Jason,* I thought. *Leave that one to me.*

"What's the sense in my making out a list for you if you don't even follow it?" I asked, starting to escalate again for the umpteenth time. But before I could spiral, I calmed myself down. After all, nothing was going to change no matter what I said. I knew that by now.

"Just get upstairs and finish room number two," I said as normally as possible. Then I sat down in my wingback chair and started deep breathing.

What was I going to do? I felt like someone "up there" was testing me. And I thought, as I always did, that I would find a way. But I never did. And nothing changed. He continued to make the same mistakes he always did—some even worse—but still I just couldn't bring myself to fire him. Luckily, in the end, I didn't have to—he quit.

Oh happy day.

That's when I hit Sullivan for the last time and ended up with Quinton, a six-foot-four hotel management student with dreadlocks and an overly dominant mother.

At the time, I was limping along with a variety of mature women who had been lent and/or recommended to me by friends. At least, I thought they were friends—but those recommendations landed me with three or four very unsuitable workers, each one hired in a moment of extreme need.

Quinton came on the scene at the same time Pearl was working for me. Pearl was a good worker, but strictly on her own terms. She was a very thin little black woman who had finally dried herself out after years of abusing drugs and alcohol. I soon realized she was passive-aggressive and wasn't fond of white people. She was in her sixties and forced to do housekeeping to earn a living—something that engendered a lot of anger in her, especially toward the people she worked for, unless they continually placated her and sympathized with her plight.

Pearl was delighted when I hired Quinton, and she immediately took him under her wing. She babied him and rolled her eyes in disgust at me whenever I asked him to take on a difficult task. She began telling me how to treat Quinton, and pretty soon her advice smacked of telling me how I should be running my B&B. She constantly reminded me of the things I was doing she didn't like; she rolled her eyes, made faces at me, came to work late, ate food while she was working, and sometimes refused to answer me. It soon created so many problems that I had to let her go.

Quinton, who had been spoiled and coddled by an over-protective mother, eventually developed a list of issues that kept him from coming to work. He was always in trouble at school, getting into fights, and making enemies who slashed his tires.

I tried to help Quinton come to terms with the chaos in his life, but to no avail. I finally gave up and made a decision that made all my employee problems vanish: I would no longer hire college students. Instead I would look for mature workers who had more experience keeping house, working in a kitchen, and taking care of a family. This worked like a charm. I found four women who met those criteria. All but one, who eventually moved out of town, stayed with me for the next three to four years, and they were the best employees I ever had.

Pain Perdu (Lost Bread)

The word "lost"(*perdu* in French) in the title of this recipe is an allusion to Jason, who, I'm afraid, never got it together.

Ingredients
2 eggs
1 cup sugar
1 tablespoon cornstarch, dissolved in a splash of water
1 cup whole milk
½ teaspoon freshly grated nutmeg
8 slices stale white bread or 6 slices thick-cut stale bread
Butter, for griddle pan
Warm maple syrup, powdered sugar, cinnamon sugar
   and/or fresh berries for topping

Instructions
Preheat nonstick griddle or skillet over medium heat. Beat eggs very well, add sugar and beat again. Add cornstarch in water and beat that in, then add milk and nutmeg. Coat bread thoroughly with egg-milk mixture. Lightly butter hot pan. Add bread to the pan and cook slowly, 3 or 4 minutes on each side, 2 to 3 slices at a time. Serve hot with your favorite toppings.

Chapter 26

THE INNKEEPER RANTS

One of the hardest things to deal with in a small business is complaints. Some are justified, but many are not. When an innkeeper does everything in her power to make her guests comfortable and give them a lovely "complimentary" breakfast in her dining room, I feel that complaining about the amount of food you're getting or the fact that you're not served a specific item with your meal is somewhat unjustified. After all, the breakfast is complimentary, and it's so much more than you would get if you were staying in a motel.

Business declined somewhat with the change in the economy in 2008, and because of that, I had to pull back on the amount of money I spent on food, beverages, and supplies. Fresh fruit is very expensive, so we eliminated it for a while and just served juice. We also eliminated bottled water, and starting serving local water in pitchers with ice (Louisville water, luckily, is some of the best I've ever tasted). But we continued to stock our guest refrigerators with sodas and put snacks and cookies out every afternoon, and we continued to serve beautiful entrees at breakfast—Belgian waffles, vegetable omelets, bacon, ham, sausage, homemade muffins, and toast. And our servings were generous.

Given all this, I was disheartened whenever negative reviews appeared online, especially on Trip Advisor. I don't think many people realize how high the overhead is in a bed and breakfast. I also don't think they realize how a negative review can hurt a small business. I have had a few, over minor infractions, that were very unforgiving—and they have been devastating.

To give you an idea of the kind of thing I'm talking about, here are some excerpts from a couple of complaints:

"What bothered me was the noise from the streets."

"I had to eat the same breakfast as my family."

"When we returned, opening the front door took ten to fifteen minutes."

"Upon leaving, we were greeted by a thundering scene of domestic strife next door."

"Parking was on the street, which the inn keeper said was 'safer' than parking behind the inn."

"Breakfast was better than some we have had, but nothing to rave about in our opinion."

And the *pièce de résistance*: "I was asked to leave in the middle of breakfast to tend to my barking dog."(He had left the dog in his room, barking incessantly. He then brought the dog to the breakfast table and sat eating his breakfast with the dog in his lap.)

Or, "I was asked to take my dog outside . . . " because his barking was bothering everyone. One day a guest left his dog in the room and didn't return for eight hours. The dog barked the whole time.

Being an innkeeper, I know that sometimes it's nearly impossible to empty and clean a room right on time, especially if the previous guest in that room leaves late. And sometimes the breakfast doesn't turn out the way we intended. Innkeepers are human; they may get busy, tired, and hungry. But because they're innkeepers, they aren't allowed to say so or also voice their complaints.

And finally, in a review of another inn, a beautiful, well-kept inn with an extremely attentive innkeeper, the guest had written thirteen paragraphs listing complaints that were obviously grossly exaggerated. The innkeeper had scratched his nose a few times while they were checking in and that was in the list of complaints. Just because this particular innkeeper had an itchy nose, does that mean it should be one of a list of complaints in a public review?

Now, I'm not saying that minor complaints should be withheld completely. I'm just saying that they should be made to the innkeeper and not dropped anonymously onto a travel site like TripAdvisor.

And further, what I would like to know is: where is the site that innkeepers can go on to post infractions and complaints about inconsiderate guests? Guests who, for instance, knock on an innkeeper's bedroom door at 12:00 A.M. asking them to come and adjust the TV? Or who call them at 11:00 P.M. for ice? Or who leave cups, dishes, and newspapers strewn all over the parlor? Or who move the furniture around and don't put it back? Or who stay up late and talk and laugh so loudly that no one can sleep? Or whose dogs bark all day and night? Or who let their dogs pee all over the carpets and relieve themselves in the back garden and don't pick it up, or who let their kids jump on the beds and furniture, breaking lamps and chair seats in the process, and leave without telling anyone about it?

A particular incident comes to mind. I had a family of four—two adults and two teenage children—stay in my beautiful suite one time for three days. When they left, we went up to the room to clean it and the entire seat of one of my overstuffed antique wingback chairs was pushed through the bottom and hanging by a couple of strings. They had broken the springs and nearly destroyed the silk damask seat covering, then left without even bothering to tell me what happened. I called and got an estimate with an upholsterer who said it would cost $350 just to fix the seat using the existing fabric.

When I called my ex-guest and told her what happened and that we were charging her $100, she told me she would not pay it and that no one in her family had broken the chair. *Guess we have a mystery on our hands*, I thought. I did not let it go. When I first started innkeeping, I probably would have backed down, not wanting to argue for fear I would lose a customer, but after a while you learn: that kind of customer you can do without. I charged her credit card and never heard from her again.

Another time, my assistant called downstairs to tell me that the towel rack in the third-floor bathroom had been ripped off of the wall. We tried to fix it but couldn't. My maintenance man was out of town, so I had to dig up another one—no easy task—to come and fix it as soon as possible. Someone was checking into the room where this particular bathroom was the next day and I needed it done by then.

The worst part about incidents like these is that the guests who did it didn't even bother to tell us, much less offer to pay for the damage. People break lamps, chairs, small table legs, glasses, and various other room items all the time at inns. I realize that sometimes it can't be helped, and that in most cases it is an innocent accident, but if we don't know about it, we may not be able to get it fixed in time for the next guest's check in—and that makes us look bad.

Yes, some accidents are unavoidable, and they certainly are not perpetrated on purpose. But I can tell you one thing: there are plenty of guests who, if the innkeeper makes a mistake, will get on the phone to the Better Business Bureau, or post a scathing (and exaggerated) review on TripAdvisor or BedandBreakfast. com in a flash. I can see complaining if the food is really bad, or if the room is dirty, or if the towels are in rags, but complaining about noise in the street or a neighbor arguing with his wife . . . that's pretty unfair. I had absolutely no control over everything that happened outside of my house. I did complain if my next-door neighbor let his grass grow to a foot or more high, or let his children run all over my property and use the front walkways for chalkboards, or if there was a very loud party after 10:00 P.M.—but I couldn't sit on the front porch and monitor everything that went on all day long.

To be sure, I had far more wonderful guests over the years who filled my guestbook on the parlor desk with glowing accounts of their visit to my inn. Or who gave me a hug on the way out as they left for home and promised to come back. Of the hundreds who entered my home, there were only handfuls who ended up disappointed—and for that I am eternally grateful.

Another innkeeper and I developed this delicious pizza. I include the recipe here as a reminder of the day Kari wiped off the numbers on the oven knob, causing me to burn my pizza because I couldn't tell what temperature the oven was set at. Also, as I started getting older and getting more vegetarian guests, I began cutting down on the amount of meat I ate and learning to increase the vegetables I used, and to make delicious vegetable dishes. This one is easy because we use store-bought pizza crusts. We frequently had groups of six to eight women come for our *Girls Get-Away* package, and they loved our vegetarian pizza—so we started serving it regularly.

Vegetarian Pizza
(serves 6-8)

Ingredients
1 whole wheat ready-made 12 in. Boboli pizza crust
olive oil
1 large Vidalia onion, sliced and caramelized
2 sweet green peppers
1 quart packaged mushrooms
3 large or 6 small tomatoes
1 small jar sliced olives
1 small package Boursin cream cheese
1 package shredded Mozzarella
Herbs to taste (basil, oregano, etc.)
sea salt to taste
Parmesan cheese to taste

Instructions
Pre-heat oven to 450 degrees. Caramelize the onions (see instructions below). Set aside. Slice vegetables according to your preference. Sauté mushrooms in olive oil. Brush pizza crust with olive oil. Spread cream cheese on top of olive oil. Sprinkle vegetables over the cream cheese, then mozzarella on top of that. Finish with herbs, a little sea salt, and parmesan. Place on a cookie sheet and pop in the oven for 8-10 minutes. Slice and serve with a Greek or Italian salad.

Can also use: pinch of thyme and black olives (preferably oil-cured), roasted eggplant, spinach, feta and tomatoes (Greek style), or sautéed with lemon juice. Instead of tomato sauce, try using pesto as a base, or pesto mixed with mayonnaise; or make a sun-dried tomato pesto with garlic, reconstituted sundried tomatoes, water and fresh basil leaves.

How to Caramelize Onions

Caramelized onions are quite easy to make. Other than time and an onion, there is not much needed to produce wonderful, deeply caramelized onions. Because of the way onion cells are lined up, how you slice up the onion will have an effect on the final product.

If you want caramelized onions that almost melt in the mouth, you will want to cut thin slices longitudinally, from the root end to the stem end. If you'd like your caramelized onion to have a little more structure and not break down so much, slice them into thin rings across the equator. If you would like smaller caramelized pieces, you can also chop or dice the onions.

Ingredients
1 large onion, sliced per your preference
2 tablespoons olive oil, butter, or a mixture of the two
Heavy pinch of salt
A teaspoon of honey, agave nectar or corn syrup

Instructions
Heat a large sauté pan over medium-low heat. Add the oil and/or butter. Once the butter has melted and is hot, add as many onions to the pan as will fit in a ½" layer in the pan. Sprinkle the salt over the onions. The salt helps to draw water and dissolved sugars out of the onion's cells. When you salt the onions at the beginning, it will take longer to achieve browning because of the extra water it draws out, but ultimately, your onions will have a much better flavor and will brown more evenly if you add the salt at the beginning of the cooking process.

Cook the onions over medium-low heat. Cooking the onions at a relatively low temperature, called sweating, allows all the water to release into the pan and then evaporate slowly. Sweating also ensures that your onions will be soft and caramelized all the way through, and not just on the outside.

Stir the onions every couple of minutes, and adjust the heat so you hear just the merest sizzle. If your pan can't hold all of the onions, add more as the ones in the pan cook down and free up more room in the pan.

Continue cooking on medium-low to low heat, stirring frequently, until the onions are soft and anywhere from honey-colored to deep brown, depending on how caramelized you want them to be.

The process can take anywhere from ten to fifteen minutes to upwards of half an hour, depending on how many onions you are cooking and your preferred level of caramelization. Don't worry; as long as you cook them slowly and stir them frequently, you will not end up with burned onions.

Chapter 27

Back North Again

In May of 2015, I finally sold my inn. By that time, Kristie had moved to Vermont. She wanted me to try and find a place close to her and her husband; she knew I would want my own place. I had to make a decision in a hurry. It all happened in a matter of three weeks. Now, when I think back on it, I have no idea how I did it so fast. I had to pack up the contents of a nearly 5,000-square-foot, three-story mansion to be moved or sold, all while dealing with banks, mortgage companies, a realtor, estate sales persons, and so on.

In order to close the deal, I had to re-plaster a couple of the walls, do some extensive work in the basement, and put on a new roof. I had recently finished tuck-pointing and refurbishing the outside of the house. I ended up using most of my escrow money from the sale for the move, which left me just enough to buy a small condo in Vermont and to pay the moving costs to get there.

I had been trying to sell my inn for several years with no luck. It would have been hard enough to sell an 1882 historic mansion at any time, but after the crash of 2008, it was almost impossible.

I had been lucky to get a break when my housekeeper and her husband had expressed an interest in buying my inn on a land contract; it was a risk for me, but I was willing to do it if we were able to pound out a contract with our lawyers which was amenable to both of us.

Unfortunately, when the deal fell through, I was left with an empty contract and thirty boxes packed to the brim and stored on the third floor of my inn. They were the boxes I had thought I was moving to Austin. They remained there for six years. I wasn't about to start unpacking all those boxes. When I took them to Vermont and finally opened them up, I was surprised and not always delighted at my discoveries. I had so much stuff with me that I had to have two big garage sales just to make enough room in the garage to get my car in before the winter snows came.

Moving to Vermont was like moving to a third-world country for me. I honestly had no idea it was such a rural state. You have to drive for blocks to find a grocery or drug store, let alone a bank or movie theater. I'd always lived in very large cities of a million or more—places where you could usually find a drug store or restaurant down at the corner. It would have been easier for me if Kristie and her husband had stayed in Austin, but they'd decided to make the move to Vermont a couple of years before I got there. So I rolled with it.

Recently, I came across an adage voiced by Bonnie Price of WomenEntrepreneur.com, which rings so true to me: "We don't retire, we reinvent ourselves." Rather than thinking of myself as "retired" again, I prefer to think of my move to Vermont as "reinventing" myself again. I am in my mid-eighties now, and I have been reinventing myself my whole life. I never faded into the woodwork! I have approached each phase of my life proactively and made sure it was the best phase yet. I have learned how to leverage my past experiences and passions to design a present that is fulfilling. I have had two very fulfilling long-term careers, and am now in the process of embarking on a third, as a writer.

I've had so many different jobs, taken so many classes, and engaged in so many activities over the years that I would have lost count if it weren't for the fact that each one was, and still is, intrinsically woven into the fabric of my life. Along the way, some folks said I was scattered in too many directions. But I never understood why someone would view taking classes that aren't totally related to one's chosen profession, or traveling, or experiencing life's various and engaging activities, as a waste of time. Everything you do prepares you for the future. Whether or not it turns out to be a waste of time depends entirely on how you look at it and what you do with it.

I am a writer now, and I love it. I spend at least three to five hours every day doing it. I have a craving for learning, and writing has turned into a passion.

You are not born with passion. It is cultivated by your interests—by what stimulates you and excites you. It's the thing that makes you want to get up early, jump out of bed, and start working. It's the thing that sustains you through hours of focused concentration, the thing that creates that "flow."

How do we go about finding this elusive thing called passion? Well, first of all, you need to take a moment to reflect. Ask yourself, *Is there something I love doing, something that keeps grabbing my attention? Something I love to read about all the time? What do I enjoy doing so much that I'd do it for free?*

After opening my inn and finding myself in control of my own time, I was able to discover that you really can make a career out of what you love to do. I have always loved to write, and yet the closest I ever got to it for most of my life was majoring in English, taking writing classes, and teaching writing skills to high school students. I did play around with writing poetry and even tried writing short stories when I was a teacher, but I never got serious about it. I taught school for twenty-five years, got a couple of degrees, wrote masters and doctoral theses, and even helped colleagues write theirs—and yet all that time, it never dawned on me that this was my passion.

I was brought up during a time when women either went to nursing school or studied to become teachers. It never dawned on me to try writing seriously until I had owned my bed and break-fast (not a passion, by the way) for fifteen years. At that point, I had everything in place, including housekeepers, gardeners, and maintenance men, and it gave me the time to explore writing as a possible third career.

The turning point in my life that led me to believe I could become a serious writer was when I spent Christmas with my daughter in Austin one year, and her boyfriend (now her husband), who is a marketing director, told me he was building a blog. I didn't even know what a blog was at the time, but since it involved writing, I became interested in what he was doing—and seeing this interest, he suggested that I try it myself. Well, that did it! I now have three blogs, and am writing for an online magazine and Examiner.com. Am I getting paid for this? Not much. But the truth is, I'd do it for nothing. In fact, all I want to do is write! After all this time, I've found my passion. And the irony? It was there all the time.

Sometimes, in order to find a job that is right for you—that you enjoy, that you're passionate about—you have to take a risk. That risk may involve time, or money, or both. And that possibil-ity will probably elicit some degree of fear in you—which can get in the way of your finding happiness and living life to the fullest. Yes, I am a risk taker, and I have been my whole life. And it hasn't always produced the best results—but at least it gave me choices and time to figure out what I was good at, what my passion was.

Your thoughts definitely affect how you view life. If you're coming from a negative place, you will undoubtedly respond to that fear in a negative way. You may have exaggerated feelings of inadequacy, worries about your performance ability, about other people's reactions, or even about issues outside your control. You will then unconsciously seek out confirmation of those negative thoughts. Conversely, if your thoughts are positive, you'll seek out positive choices and expect positive results.

I have found that my reality is influenced by the degree to which I approach life positively or negatively. Negativity *is* reality to the negative thinker. Her thoughts make it so. The positive thinker, on the other hand, may also see reality, but she sees it in a different light. Being a positive thinker doesn't make me reject or ignore reality, thinking that just because I approach life in a positive way, my problems will disappear. Rather, it allows me to look at my problems in a different light—to look for creative solutions and choose to act in positive ways.

I like to think that by this time I can call myself a gourmet cook, especially when it comes to breakfast. At my inn, we always served the very best breakfast we could afford, with the freshest ingredients. We usually served two courses, with fruit and bread (sweet or savory) first, along with coffee or tea. We followed that with a hot entrée, fresh ground coffee, and a sweet of some sort.

We alternated savory egg & vegetable dishes with sweet selections. Some of the favorites were spinach-herb quiche, eggs Benedict, or Denver omelets. And for sweet dishes, my guests loved our Grand Marnier French toast, baked Dutch Baby pancakes, or Belgium waffles with fresh strawberries and whipped cream.

We tried to be creative with our fruit dishes and perfected three guest favorites: baked Ginger peaches, heavenly bananas, and pears in white Zinfandel. The pears in white Zinfandel recipe was featured in the latest Kentucky Bed and Breakfast Association cookbook. I have included my scrambled egg method and recipe on the following page:

Recipe

Scrambled Eggs

I loved trying new things, like Gâteau of Vegetable Crepes, Spinach-herb Quiches, Croissants au Gratin, and Tarragon Eggs in Puff Pastry. All are wonderful gourmet dishes. Most of my guests loved them, but every now and then, a guest (or two, or three) just wants down home biscuits and gravy, or plain old scrambled eggs. Well, I could do that too. In fact, I've had the scrambled-egg thing down pat.

When I first started making breakfast for eight to ten people on a regular basis, I discovered I needed a few menus that would be easy to do for a large group, or in a situation where my help didn't show up, or when I had come downstairs late in the morning, with only ten minutes to get it all together. Or maybe I forgot to go shopping and the only ingredients I had dictated the kind of breakfast I could make. I most often had eggs on hand. I was never big on fried or poached eggs, so I spent most of my time perfecting the scrambled egg.

Most people like scrambled eggs, adults and kids alike. Some like them plain, some with cheese, and some with ketchup or chili sauce. Some even like sautéed mushrooms, tomatoes, or spinach stirred in. Kids seemed to prefer them plain or with cheese. They didn't want cream cheese, or feta, or mozzarella. They wanted plain old American or, maybe, mild cheddar. I could do that, but my specialty was scrambled eggs with cream cheese, onion, chives, basil, and dill.

Here is my take on "gourmet" eggs. They are fabulous! And my guests, except for some of the kids, love them. I get a lot of positive feedback. Besides liking the flavor and ingredients of the eggs, they also like the consistency and the appearance. To me, making scrambled eggs correctly is an art. When I was first exploring the best way to prepare them, a fellow innkeeper suggested microwaving them. I tried it and they did puff up nicely and look appetizing, but they were rather insipid. For some reason, the microwave cooked the flavor right out of them. I wanted more control, and the only way to get it is with a heavy, seasoned, wrought-iron frying pan and a rubber spatula.

There are several things you must and must not do when preparing scrambled eggs. First of all, if you cook for over four people, you should mix them in the blender but for not too long. You want air in them, but you don't want them to be overly foamy. Secondly, never water them down with milk or even cream. Next, before you cook them, always melt a liberal amount of butter in the pan and have the pan very hot—not too hot, you don't want the butter to turn brown. Test the pan with a sprinkle of cold water. If it sizzles, you're ready to add the beaten eggs.

Now—and this is one of the most important parts—start with the flame on high, but gradually lower it as you slowly cook the eggs. Scrambling does not mean swishing the eggs around furiously in circles. The proper motion is a pushing motion, back and forth slowly, as the eggs begin to coagulate. Be sure you're scraping all the way to the bottom of the pan.

If you're cooking for kids, try using shredded cheddar cheese. I hate American cheese! Do not add the cheese until the eggs are almost finished. You don't want them too wet or too dry. They should look like little yellow mounds of whipped cream, only they will be more firm. As you're finishing up, the cheese will be melting. Fold it in carefully.

Now, if you're doing the cream cheese version, start out the same way. Sprinkle on the herbs as the eggs begin to coagulate, then add three or four large dabs of Philadelphia cream cheese with chives and onions. Place the cheese in different places around the pan, so it will be easier to work in and distribute.

If your eggs finish before your family or guests are ready to eat, you may leave them in the hot pan and cover with tinfoil until ready to serve. If they will be sitting in the pan a while, don't finish them completely. You don't want them to get hard in the hot pan. You want them firm but not hard or, on the other hand, wet and runny. Serve your eggs with ham, bacon or sausage and hot buttered toast, biscuits or croissants. Do not let them get cold. Cold scrambled eggs are terrible!

Chapter 28

WOULD I DO IT AGAIN?

Would I do it again? Hell yeah . . . in a New York minute, as they say! In all the years I've lived and worked, I have never learned so much about myself than I did in the twenty years I spent as an innkeeper. And for me, my life from age forty on has been a continual reflection on who and what I am. Before then it was something of a floating opera: lots of drama, little real stability.

For a good deal of my childhood, my father was sleeping and my mother was sick. So what I learned about life, I learned through a series of trials and errors. I found out early on that I could figure out the answer to most logistical problems; my biggest challenge has always been how to tackle social interactions. I was never taught how to get along with others, and as a child the only working model I had to emulate was my grandmother, the rock of the family.

Since I developed very few social skills in my early years, my defenses kicked in and by my teens I had begun not to care about being socially correct. I would even go to the other extreme. There were times here and there when I tried to fit in, but it just took too much energy and thought. In the end, I would find myself blurting out remarks that, after receiving negative reactions, I was sorry for.

So, as I said, I floated through the early part of my life, and I ended up marrying someone with social skills only slightly better than mine. I guess I felt we could face the socially adept together.

When that marriage failed, I tried it a second and then a third time. But frankly, I didn't like being married one bit. Finally, I decided therapy was in order—and it was the smartest choice I ever made. I found the parent I never had in my therapist, and began to understand why sometimes you need to just go along with the program. I discovered that I was afraid to let go of control, and so I disagreed with everyone and trusted no one. Furthermore, I was drawn to relationships that reinforced my neuroses.

Going back to school and getting a teaching degree was another smart move. As I gradually began to care, I discovered what an overachiever I was. I threw myself into my studies and ended up on the Dean's List every single semester. However, I had two young children at home, and my mothering skills were really lacking. Why wouldn't they be? I had never had much mothering myself. What did I know about being a good mother? Besides, I was too busy building up my own ego.

Eventually, this began to change, and I had to start dealing with the guilt of having put myself before my two daughters. I had rationalized it by telling myself that building a career for myself would give us financial stability—which it did. But they needed more from me.

When I started teaching for the Chicago public school system, I launched into an in-depth reinventing of who I was. It was not something that was in my conscious mind at first. It started happening when I discovered that I was good at teaching and that my students were actually achieving and benefiting from their relationships with me. This transferred into my personal life, and I started taking being a mother more seriously.

By that time, my daughters were teenagers. As I struggled to build a stronger connection with each of them, the old adage "I've become my mother" hit me hard. Like my own mother, I hadn't been there for my children during their formative years—and for one of my daughters, it was too late. Our relationship was damaged and could never be repaired, even though I tried for years. My younger daughter escaped unscathed, however, and over the years we have become the best of friends.

Besides building up my ego and self-confidence, teaching school further instilled in me the love for learning that I had always felt since I was a child. It also required me to develop crackerjack planning and organizational skills—a necessity when you're responsible for almost two hundred students. I soon became aware of what a perfectionist I was. When I started working with students with cognitive and behavioral problems, I identified some of the same behaviors and processes in myself. The main one was that I am slightly OCD. My training as a specialist in cognitive disorders taught me how to work on myself and develop strategies that allowed me to use my shortcomings to my advantage.

All these experiences transferred to Louisville and running my bed and breakfast. Yes, I took a risk going into a business I knew absolutely nothing about, but somewhere in my psyche I knew I had the smarts and the wherewithal to do the job. I was confident that those traits—combined with my love of cooking, my ability to learn quickly, my tenacity, and my having been an art student and a teacher—would carry me through to success. At the same time, I was aware that I had shortcomings that I would have to overcome or somehow make work for me. I was asocial, I was unfamiliar with the Internet, and I was sixty-four years old. I was a perfectionist with OCD tendencies, I'd never been an employer, and I had very little money to get started.

Like I had done all my life, however, I dove in and did whatever I had to do to get my business off and running. I learned about the Victorian period—the food, the decor, the ambiance.

I started collecting recipes for breakfast dishes and learned to modify them, as well as coming up with some of my own. I learned about special diets for guests who couldn't eat sugar, eggs, wheat, or strawberries, among other things (I had no idea there were so many people who were allergic to so many foods); and I learned to shop wisely and frugally, store food properly, keep accurate records, train housekeepers and assistants, and deal with disgruntled guests and mishaps without going into panic mode. That, and so much more. I was in "learning" heaven. I loved it. It appealed to the overachiever residing within me.

Overcoming the challenges and solving the many problems inherent in running a small business rarely got me down. In fact, they turned me on—sent me straight into the "I can do this" mode I loved. The only problem that I found really taxing was the one that small business owners are continually confronted with: cash flow. At first, I hated not knowing when my next booking would be. Eventually I learned to live with it, though I never did grow to like it.

It was hard during the economic crunch that hit us in 2008. But it got better as time went on. I never had 60 percent occupancy again, like I had my third through tenth years in business, but I stayed around 45 percent, and that was okay. Of course, I had a teacher's pension, which helped. Without it, I probably couldn't have made it. Statistics have shown that in order to make a living (without a second income) running a bed and breakfast, you need more than five guestrooms—and I only had four, except during the times I would rent out my own room and sleep on a rollaway in the back hallway.

During the last six or seven years I owned and ran my business, I began writing again on a regular basis, sometimes four to five hours a day. It all started when my son-in-law suggested I build a blog for my bed and breakfast. I had no idea what a blog was, except to hear Rosie O Donnell talk about the comments she was getting on hers that she didn't like, and how she had decided to shut it down. And soon after that, the *Julie and Julia* blog appeared, and blogs began to pop up all over the place.

I became intrigued with the idea and asked him to explain the concept to me and to show me how to set up a blog of my own, which he did. I decided it should be centered on my bed and breakfast and what went on there. I named it *Inn Notes: a Bed and Breakfast Blog* , and wrote about everything I could think of. Amazingly enough, I never ran out of ideas for posts. I discovered I was a natural. And so I constructed my second blog, *Inn Business*, a blog about the hospitality industry. Again, I had more ideas for posts than I had time to write. And I loved it. I became obsessed, as I am wont to do when I find something I'm really good at.

During the time I first engaged in blogging, I became interested in social media and joined Twitter and Facebook. By that time, I had discovered a site where I could publish journal articles and make a little money at the same time. There were thousands of writers on the site, so I could also get some feedback on my writing. I found several sites like this and joined them all. I tried writing fiction, but quickly returned to non-fiction where I was comfortable and could put out at a high rate. I soon started writing for two online magazines, *Examiner.com* and *Eye on Life*, as well as *Pink* and *Open Salon*. All the while, my writing was improving and I was writing more and more each day, even though I was still running the business full-time, but now with lots of help.

I then started my third blog, *Business and Creative Women's Forum*, and was entertaining the idea of starting a fourth one. It was this continual blogging that made me gradually aware of how comfortable I was with non-fiction, especially stream of consciousness and personal essays in the first person. I realized that it was now time to start the memoir I'd been thinking about for a few years—the one that would tell the stories I had been collecting for years about my innkeeping experiences. I had previously started posting them on one of my writing sites under the name

Tales from an Innkeeper's Crypt. I soon had a pretty good following, and they kept wondering what was going to happen next and asking when I was going to turn my collected stories into a book.

And so one day it began. I let it all hang out, and the words just poured out onto the pages. All that blogging had helped me find my *voice*, but it needed more work. I had the memoir nearly finished when I realized I needed to rewrite it to make sure my voice was coming through loud and clear, especially in a couple of chapters I wasn't sure about.

I was getting plenty of feedback by that time from both alpha and beta readers. I started focusing on how I was going to publish it and that made me think about my platform. I had a pretty good start on it, with all the writing sites I was on, the online magazines I wrote for, my blogs, and the many social media sites I had joined. In addition, I had names of hundreds of guests who had visited my inn. At this point, I have nearly 500 followers on Facebook and nearly 1200 on Twitter. But you can never have too many people behind you, especially if you plan to publish a book. It was time for another blog, one about writing.

I constructed a new blog and named it *A Memorable Time of My Life,* which in reality it was. This blog would be for and about writers. I wrote, researched, and contacted other writers who would be willing to guest post. I wanted as many tips and how-tos about writing as I could collect in one place. In addition, I would post excerpts from my memoir to generate interest among my readers and maybe get some additional feedback. This blog is the most popular of all four and has more followers than the others, probably because I promote it the most.

From working for a large public school system, of which I was only a small part, to becoming the sole owner of a small business was quite a stretch, especially without any prior business experience. But instead of perceiving the anxiety I felt at the beginning as fear, I chose to open myself up and embrace it as excitement—a whoosh of life rushing through my body, whisking me off into new places filled with lovely challenges, all of which made me stronger and more confident. I was never happier and more satisfied in my entire life as I was when I ran my inn.

The following is one of my favorite recipes. It is easy to make and so delicious, and my guests loved it.

Tomato and Goat Cheese Tart
(Serves: 6-8)

Ingredients
1 homemade or store-bought pie crust
5-6 medium tomatoes, sliced thick and squeezed gently to
remove the pulp
1 cup goat cheese, mascarpone, or a mixture of the two
1 tablespoon chopped fresh rosemary
1 teaspoon sea salt
Optional: 1 teaspoon grated lemon zest

Instructions
Preheat oven to 350 degrees.

Line a 9" pie with pie crust. Let the edges drape down the outside of the pie pan a little for a more rustic look. Use a fork to poke a few holes in the bottom of the crust.

In a small bowl, mix goat cheese, mascarpone, rosemary, sea salt and optional lemon zest. Spread over the bottom of the pie.

Layer tomatoes over the cheese mixture until pie is completely full. Sprinkle with a little sea salt.

Bake for 35-40 minutes, or until crust is light brown and tomatoes are soft. If crust is browning too quickly, cover with a piece of aluminum foil.

Remove from oven and let cool for at least 1 hour.

RECIPE INDEX

In order of appearance:

ABOUT THE AUTHOR

Nancy Hinchliff holds undergraduate degrees in music and education and graduate degrees in music, science of education, and special education. She is certified to teach English, music, geography and history. She taught in the Chicago public school system for twenty-five years, and in the school of education at the University of Illinois in Chicago. She has been writing all of her adult life—mostly journal articles, essays, and creative non-fiction—and has been published in newsletters, local magazines, and as a guest on several blogs. In 2008 she coauthored *Room at the Table,* a cookbook written for the Bed and Breakfast Association of Kentucky, for which she won their president's award. Hinchliff is now a member of the Burlington, VT Writer's Workshops and is working on her second memoir.

Author photo © Kim Hollister

SELECTED TITLES FROM SHE WRITES PRESS

She Writes Press is an independent publishing company founded to serve women writers everywhere. Visit us at www.shewritespress.com.

Gap Year Girl by Marianne Bohr. $16.95, 978-1-63152-820-0. Thirty-plus years after first backpacking through Europe, Marianne Bohr and her husband leave their lives behind and take off on a yearlong quest for adventure.

Daring to Date Again: A Memoir by Ann Anderson Evans. $16.95, 978-1-63152-909-2. A hilarious, no-holds-barred memoir about a legal secretary turned professor who dives back into the dating pool headfirst after twelve years of celibacy.

Peanut Butter and Naan: Stories of an American Mother in The Far East by Jennifer Magnuson. $16.95, 978-1-63152-911-5. The hilarious tale of what happened when Jennifer Magnuson moved her family of seven from Nashville to India in an effort to shake things up—and got more than she bargained for.

Renewable: One Woman's Search for Simplicity, Faithfulness, and Hope by Eileen Flanagan. $16.95, 978-1-63152-968-9. At age forty-nine, Eileen Flanagan had an aching feeling that she wasn't living up to her youthful ideals or potential, so she started trying to change the world—and in doing so, she found the courage to change her life.

Tasting Home: Coming of Age in the Kitchen by Judith Newton. $16.95, 978-1-938314-03-2. An extraordinary journey through the cuisines, cultures, and politics of the 1940s through 2011, complete with recipes.

Dumped: Stories of Women Unfriending Women edited by Nina Gaby. $16.95, 978-1-63152-954-2. Candid, relatable stories by established and emerging women writers about being discarded by someone from whom they expected more: a close female friend.

CPSIA information can be obtained
at www.ICGtesting.com
Printed in the USA
FSOW01n0809040217
30290FS